LUDWIG WITTGENSTEIN
A Student's Memoir

Ludwig Wittgenstein
A Student's Memoir

Theodore Redpath

Duckworth

First published in 1990 by
Gerald Duckworth & Co. Ltd.
The Old Piano Factory
43 Gloucester Crescent, London NW1

ISBN 0 7156 2329 X

British Library Cataloguing in Publication Data

Redpath, Theodore
  Ludwig Wittgenstein : a student's memoir.
  1. English philosophy. Wittgenstein, Ludwig, 1889–1951
  I. Title
  192

ISBN 0-7156-2329-X

Photoset in North Wales by
Derek Doyle & Associates, Mold, Clwyd.
Printed in Great Britain by
Billing & Son Limited, Worcester

Contents

Contents

Preface

It was about ten years ago that I had the idea of gathering together some stray reminiscences of Wittgenstein the man as I encountered him over fifty years ago in his 'lectures' (better called 'seminars' or 'classes') and then at various times outside his teaching hours. I laid the work aside several times because of other projects on which I was engaged, and I had little time and insufficient facilities to concentrate effectively enough to carry it forward between 1980 and 1987, when I was abroad on Visiting Professorships in France, Germany, Japan and the USA. I had not even thought of taking the work up again in 1988, and had actually forgotten that Wittgenstein had been born in 1889 and that his centenary year was hard upon us, though I was stimulated by a talk about Wittgenstein with my old friend Robin Jasper[1] in Sussex in September 1988.

The actual reminder of the centenary came to me in October 1988 from my colleague and friend Dr Bela Bollobas, Fellow of Trinity College and Reader in Pure Mathematics in the University. He asked me if I would be willing to take part in a BBC film of interviews and other material about Wittgenstein to be made by Christopher Sykes Productions. I discussed the project

[1] Robin Jasper, CMG, a retired diplomat, who was a contemporary of mine at Cambridge, where he was a Classical Scholar of Clare College.

7

with Christopher Sykes and his assistant Emma Crichton-Miller and gladly took a small part in their interesting film. I was also lucky that the first volume of Brian McGuinness's splendid biography[2] dealing with even earlier years was published in 1988. This book aroused my interest in Wittgenstein's ancestry and early life and has provided invaluable background.

Once made aware of the centenary, I began to roam through memories of Wittgenstein as he had appeared to me when I was young. I remembered many moments vividly, but I sometimes had difficulty assigning accurate dates to them. I have since been helped in this by recollections of friends and colleagues, and by recourse to documentary evidence, including occasional letters and other material relating to Wittgenstein which I have extracted from a hoard of miscellaneous papers accumulated over the years.

For permission to use copyright material I am grateful to the following: Trinity College Cambridge, Cecilia Sjögren, Tim Smiley and the Cambridge University Moral Science Club, and the present successors of the publishers of the 1933 edition of *Tractatus Logico-Philosophicus*, Routledge, Chapman and Hall.

I wish to express my thanks to the following for information and help of various kinds, without imputing to them responsibility for any errors that may appear in the book: Elizabeth Anscombe, Joan Bevan, Bela Bollobas, Robin Jasper, Alice Ambrose (Lazerowitz), Casimir Lewy, Michael Nedo, John Oates, Robin O'Neill, Maurice Wilkes, John Wisdom, Georg Henrik von Wright, Tom Wyatt. For her secretarial skill and care,

[2] *Wittgenstein, A Life: Young Ludwig 1889-1921*, London 1988.

and her willing and intelligent help, I am enormously grateful to Diana Piggott.

Finally, I thank my wife for her encouragement and for her eagle-eyed help with the proofs.

Cambridge
July 1989   T.R.

1

I first came across the name 'Ludwig Wittgenstein' when I was about sixteen. I was staying for the school holidays with my parents in a hotel in Eastbourne. My mother had been badly injured in a motor accident there and was now slowly convalescing.

Among the books I had brought away to read during the holidays was Herbert Read's *English Prose Style*. I can well remember the early morning before breakfast when I was reading that book in bed and, in the chapter called 'The Paragraph', on turning over from page 59 to 60, I suddenly saw the short numbered paragraphs 6.4312 – 7.0 from the end of Wittgenstein's *Tractatus Logico-Philosophicus*,[1] which Read quoted as an 'extreme example' of 'the use of paragraphs as a schematic device to give emphasis to the transitions of thought'. As I read these 'paragraphs' I was spellbound. I did not altogether forget that they were being quoted as a very special example of 'English prose style', but I was also fascinated by the philosophical content. As some of my readers will know, what the printed page faced me with was this:

6.4312   The solution of the riddle of life in space and time lies *outside* space and time.

6.432   *How* the world is, is completely indifferent for what is higher. God does not reveal

[1] This was the printed page as it faced me in Herbert Read, *English Prose Style*, London 1928. The text in the English translation, London 1933, differs in a few places.

himself in the world.

6.4321   The facts all belong only to the task and not to its performance.

6.44   Not *how* the world is, is the mystical, but *that* it is.

6.45   The contemplation of the world *sub specie aeterni* is its contemplation as a limited whole.
           The feeling of the world as a limited whole is the mystical feeling.

6.5   For an answer which cannot be expressed the question too cannot be expressed.
           The *riddle* does not exist.
           If a question can be put at all, then it *can* also be answered.

6.51   Scepticism is *not* irrefutable, but palpably senseless, if it would doubt where a question cannot be asked.
           For doubt can only exist where there is a question; a question only where there is an answer, and this only where something *can* be *said*.

6.52   We feel that even if *all possible* scientific questions can be answered, the problems of life have still not been touched at all. Of course there is then no question left, and just this is the answer.

6.521   The solution of the problem of life is seen in the vanishing of this problem.

6.522   There is indeed the inexpressible. This *shows* itself; it is the mystical.

6.53   The right method of philosophy would be this: to say nothing except what can be said, i.e. something that has nothing to do with philosophy: and then always, when someone also wished to say something metaphysical, to demonstrate to him that he had given no meaning to certain signs in his propositions. This method would be unsatisfying to the other – he would not have the feeling that we were teaching philosophy – but it would be the only strictly correct method.

6.54   My propositions are elucidatory in this way: he who understands me finally recognises them as senseless, when he has climbed out through them, on them, over them. (He must, so to speak, throw away the ladder after he has climbed up on it.)
He must surmount these propositions; then he sees the world rightly.

7   Whereof one cannot speak, thereof one must be silent.

I was far from understanding all these propositions, or 'observations', as it would perhaps be safer to call them. But some of them seemed to mean something both intelligible and exciting to me. I had already started to read some philosophy at school. One of the masters had lent me Russell's stimulating little Home University Library book, *The Problems of Philosophy*, and I had read some of the *De Officiis* and a part of the *Republic*. I had, however, little idea of the depth of meaning of some of Wittgenstein's sentences, though 6.44, 'Not *how* the world is, is the mystical, but *that* it is', struck home to me at once, and it has often occurred to me since and made me pause to think about it. The metaphor of the ladder also fascinated me, though it was not until much later that I began to appreciate how the metaphor worked in the philosophical context. The final sentence, in its oracular grandeur, also impressed me, though I believe it rather served for me as a caution against big talk about deep things than as something more precise. There was, however, also a more general impression that I received from this series of observations. On the one hand they seemed to me to be hard-headed, anti-metaphysical; on the other they seemed to express a deep respect for 'the mystical' and to suggest that 'the problems of life' were really not *less* but *more* important than the scientific questions to which Wittgenstein was saying that there must be scientific answers.

Yet, curiously enough, though the impact on me of this page-and-a-half from Wittgenstein was sufficiently strong to make it very unlikely that I should forget the name of the writer, I made no attempt to follow up this memorable experience. Many other impressions were impinging on my mind. My schoolmasters, in their several ways, were interesting me in literature – Greek, Roman, French, German and English – and in mathematics, and I had no intention at that time of reading philosophy at university. That piece of Wittgenstein indeed remained in my mind rather as a powerful piece of *writing*: muscular, tough and yet evasively mysterious.

2

About two years later, in 1931, I went up to Cambridge as an undergraduate. After much heart-searching I had decided to read English, having seriously intended to read Modern Languages (French and Italian). I had been entered for Gonville and Caius and had been exempted from the College entrance exam by the Senior Tutor, Arnold McNair (later famous as one of the Judges of the International Court at The Hague). I had, however, at that time something of a tenor voice, and I was fortunate enough to win a Choral Exhibition at St Catharine's which was open to me a year before I intended to enter the University. At Cambridge I read both Parts of the English Tripos.

During a good part of my undergraduate career Wittgenstein was in Cambridge, but I cannot remember once hearing his name mentioned. In my final year I read, under Basil Willey, for the so-called 'English Moralists' paper in Part II of the English Tripos, and I went to relevant lectures in the English Faculty, and also to some in the Faculty of Classics (Cornford, Guthrie, Baldry) and in the Faculty of Moral Science (Broad), and I became again interested in philosophy; but, though Wittgenstein was undoubtedly lecturing at that time in his rooms in Trinity, I was totally unaware of it, and even of his presence in Cambridge. In retrospect I am not in the least sorry. I had quite enough to interest me, under the guidance of my admirable Tutor and Director of Studies, Tom Henn. What is more, without greater familiarity than I had at that time with the work of earlier philosophers, both ancient and modern, I do not think I could possibly have learnt what I did, at a later stage, from Wittgenstein's way of philosophising.

3

After I took Part II of the English Tripos I was keen to spend some years in philosophical study, and my father and I went to see Broad and arranged with him that I should plan to sit Part II of the Moral Sciences Tripos the next year. I spent most of the Long Vacation reading the works Broad suggested: Descartes's *Meditations*, Spinoza's *Ethics*, Leibniz's *Monadology*, Locke's *Essay*, Hume's *Treatise of Human Nature*, Kant's *Critique of Pure*

15

Reason and commentaries on each of them. I was enthralled with the work, especially when I *seemed* to understand it tolerably well, as with Descartes, Leibniz, Locke and Hume. Spinoza I found very hard to grasp, and Kant, though not so formidably obscure as I had imagined, sometimes had me thoroughly beat.

At the start of the Michaelmas Term a most important thing happened to me. I was sent for by Ivor (I.A.) Richards, of Magdalene, who had been one of my Examiners in Part II of the English Tripos. He told me that he had asked to see me because the Examiners had liked my papers and, now that I had switched to Moral Sciences, he wanted me to go to see him once a week during Full Term, without any fee, to discuss philosophy. I accepted this generous offer with alacrity, and I had many stimulating talks with Richards over the next two years. It would of course be irrelevant to the purpose of this book to say anything in detail about those talks. What *is* extremely relevant on the other hand, is that the very first time I went to see Richards he told me that one thing I must start doing as soon as possible was to attend Wittgenstein's lectures. He told me that these lectures were not held in a lecture room but in Wittgenstein's own rooms in Trinity – that Wittgenstein lived liked a saint, that he was 'beautiful', but that he wore himself out during the course of a term's lecturing and that the ravages the effort made on him were terrible.

I had no idea what Wittgenstein really looked like, or even how old he was. I did buy a copy of the parallel text of the *Tractatus*, however, and read a good deal of the German text as well as the English. This helped to make me imagine the author as a kind of prophet, and I endowed him with the facial appearance of a 'prophet', with a thin long sensitive, El Grecoish kind of face, framed by long strands of silvery hair and set with large, dark, expressive eyes.

I had already firmly decided to follow Wittgenstein's course of lectures and, when the afternoon came on which the first was to be given, I mounted the stone steps of G staircase in Whewell's Court, Trinity, to Wittgenstein's rooms on the top floor, shortly before 5 o'clock. I knocked on the door. I can't remember whether anyone told me to go in, but I did. My surprise at what I saw was considerable. There must have been about two dozen people in the room, some standing, some sitting, either on deck-chairs with light-green canvas material backs, or on upright garden chairs with similar green material backs and seats. Everyone was waiting for five o'clock, when the lecture was due to start. On the mantelshelf, on which there was a small blackboard, I noticed a dark blue octavo book with the spine turned towards the audience. On the spine in gold letters were the words *Augustinus: Confessiones*. Wittgenstein himself was sitting on one of the deckchairs near the stone mantelshelf. He was bent forward, with his elbows resting on his knees and his hands pressed against each other with the fingers outstretched, almost as if he were praying. He was looking slightly downwards, and I noticed the fine form of his eyelids. His eyebrows were raised, and his forehead in consequence was slightly furrowed. He was wearing a brown sports jacket, with a light-brown jersey underneath. He was not wearing a tie. The whole impression of his dress was simple, tidy and clean. Out of the upper left pocket of his jacket there protruded a leather watch strap, fastened into the buttonhole by a crossbar. (This was to play a part in a typical episode which I shall be describing later.) Wittgenstein's hair was utterly different from what I had imagined. It was cut fairly short and gave his head something of a military aspect. Its colour was iron-grey from fairish. I was also wrong about the colour of his eyes. When, on the dot of five, he sprang to his feet and, resting an arm on the mantelshelf, turned to his audience and began the lecture, one was impressed by the alertness of his face and the intense gaze of his clear blue eyes. His demeanour struck me as imperious, and he seemed to me to look more like an active general than the mystical philosopher whose appearance I had concocted in the crannies of my brain.

This first lecture consisted largely of a disclaimer that he proposed to impart to his audience metaphysical 'truths', or indeed that he would be concerned to transmit knowledge at all, in the sense in which this could be said of a geographer or a physicist. If that was what any member of the audience was expecting he would be disappointed. What the lectures *would* be offering was, according to Wittgenstein, more like the work of a *masseur*. If anyone happened to be suffering from a particular kind of mental cramp, Wittgenstein might be able to help him. What this meant was at the time somewhat obscure to me. It probably helped to discourage some of those who had come to this first lecture from coming to any more of them. It is very likely that he deliberately intended this. He often said that he didn't want any 'tourists' at his lectures. At all events the audience at the second lecture had dropped to about twelve or fifteen, and my impression is that about ten or twelve of us attended regularly for the rest of the academical year. This meant four or five hours each week – 2-2½ hours on two afternoons per week – Tuesdays and Fridays, I think: certainly not Thursdays, when Moore had his At Homes at his house in Chesterton Road.

I attended Wittgenstein's lectures from 1934 to 1936 and again from 1938 to 1940, when I joined the Army. I find it hard to remember exactly who attended during that first year; but I well remember *some* of those who were there. There was, for instance, the very charming and intelligent American mathematician and logician Alice Ambrose (later Alice Lazerowitz, and, like her husband Morris, a Professor at Smith College); there was another pleasant American, Abraham Gans; there was the Trinity mathematician Francis Skinner, Wittgenstein's closest friend in Cambridge at that time; there was George Paul, who had done brilliantly at St Andrews and was equally successful at Cambridge. (Paul ultimately became a philosophy don at Oxford where he remained until his tragic death some years later by drowning in a sailing accident.) There was also Rush Rhees, who was a Research Student, working on Brentano, and who was to work intensively on Wittgenstein's philosophy over many years and later to become one of his three literary heirs. I think R.L. Goodstein of Magdalene, a mathematician, was also there. He later became a Professor and wrote a volume of essays on the foundations of mathematics; and I believe Charles Hardie, also of Magdalene and also a mathematician, was already in the audience. In addition I am pretty certain that A.G.M. Landau of Trinity, another mathematician, was there, and also Alister Watson, a young mathematical Fellow of King's who later went into the Admiralty. John Wisdom, later Professor of Philosophy at Cambridge, was there, also Peter Dupré, later in medical practice. Wisdom, whom I later got to know well, had been appointed as my Supervisor for Part II of the Moral Sciences Tripos. He was very stimulating.

Wittgenstein's style of lecturing was quite unlike anything I had come across. Richards had told me rather enigmatically that 'sometimes something happens, sometimes it doesn't', and I had also read in the Preface to Broad's *Five Types of Ethical Theory* of 'the highly syncopated pipings of Herr Wittgenstein's flute'. I was therefore not wholly unprepared to find Wittgenstein's lectures unconventional in form. I had not realised, however, how personal and, in some important sense, 'natural' they would be. During a good part of the year, I think, the topic was the foundations of mathematics, and though this was not a topic with which I was very familiar I tried to make myself better able to understand it by reading Russell's *Introduction to Mathematical Philosophy* and his Introduction to *Principia Mathematica*.[2] This helped me to warm to the subject, and I began to appreciate some of the subtle points which Wittgenstein made. Quite often these points were sparked off by remarks made by members of the audience at his invitation. For his own train of thought would frequently come to a halt. On such occasions he would sometimes sit astride a small upright chair, resting his arms on the back or holding the tops of the uprights, and curse himself roundly in such terms as 'Damn my bloody soul!' Sometimes, on the other hand, he would shout out 'Help me, someone!', and then some member of the audience might make a suggestion. If he thought there was something in it, he would encourage the speaker to continue by 'Yes, go on!', said tentatively, and with the typical gesture of pushing his hands, flat against each other with outstretched fingers, towards the speaker. On the other hand if he didn't think the suggestion useful he would often dismiss it with a sharp downward movement of one of his hands and arms. He seldom had any notes for his lectures – just occasionally a scrap of paper or an envelope. He never wore a gown or expected anyone in the audience to wear one. From time to time he would use the blackboard, e.g. for truth functions, or for proposi-

---

[2] It was only later that I read through both Russell's *Foundations of Geometry* and his *Principles of Mathematics*.

tions in symbolic logic, or for numbers or series. He seldom wrote up anything technically complicated. His manner of speaking was usually slow and his use of English simple but resourceful. He could be very pungent. For example, I remember 'Civilisation, or whatever you call the bloody thing!' The lilt of his voice, and his gestures, were very infectious. Several members of his audience (including myself) began to pick up his mannerisms. (He later told me that he was aware that he had himself picked up mannerisms of speech and gesture from Frege.)

It was a long time before I felt able to say anything in response to the call 'Help me, someone!', and I am not sure that I ever did during that first term. In any case before the end of 1934 I decided to change my own plan of study. I did not feel that I would have been able to pick up enough philosophy in less than a year to make a reasonable showing in Part II of the Moral Sciences Tripos, but I still wanted to spend some years in philosophical study. In any case I had already taken my BA degree. I therefore decided to abandon Part II at the end of the academical year and apply instead forthwith for admission as a Research Student in the Faculty of Moral Science. On my academic record, and with the backing of my Supervisor and of Broad, I was admitted. I decided to work on Leibniz, whose great philosophical system seemed to me of absorbing interest. What I vaguely wanted to do was to try to discuss it in what might be called 'Cambridge terms' – that is, by scrutinising closely the basic concepts and the language of the propositions of Leibniz's system – and to indicate in detail what turns he had taken conceptually and linguistically in order to construct that wonderful metaphysical edifice.[3] (In course of time my scheme

[3] Incidentally, I remember Broad saying in one of his lectures that Leibniz's metaphysical system was the only system he knew of which might possibly be true.

21

underwent several modifications, but that remained the
guiding idea.) Broad, who knew a great deal about
Leibniz, and indeed about the history of philosophy in
general, was appointed my Supervisor.

4

During the next two terms at Wittgenstein's lectures
(Lent and Easter 1935) I must have made some
contributions to the discussions from time to time,
because I heard from one or two friends in the class who
knew Wittgenstein personally that he had been kind
enough to say that he liked some of the points I had
made. Then one day he actually asked me to stay behind
after one of his lectures. I did so, and he enquired what
topic I was researching on. When I told him that I was
working on some of the metaphysical controversies in
which Leibniz was engaged, he said he was sorry that I
was working on a subject in the history of philosophy
rather than on a topic in philosophy itself. As this seemed
at variance with Broad's view that I had some special
talent for the history of philosophy and should
concentrate on that, I was rather perplexed. Moreover I
didn't feel that I could change my course of research,
although I felt that it could have been very attractive to
work on a non-historical topic, partly because it would
probably have involved less reading and more thinking,
and partly because there were a number of such topics
which interested me. I did, on the other hand, feel
warmed by Wittgenstein's remark, which seemed to me
something of a compliment.

Indeed what he said encouraged me to be somewhat
bolder in risking suggestions when he called for them,

and I cannot pretend that I was not gratified when some suggestions of mine were rewarded by his making a comment such as 'Well, I must confess, that takes the biscuit', though by no means all my suggestions were favourably received and I had sometimes to undergo the dismissive sweep of the arm which plainly indicated that one was barking up the wrong tree. On one occasion during the Easter Term 1935, however, I was so stimulated by a discussion that took place on a topic concerning a numerical series that I wrote a short piece of a few pages on a knotty problem that seemed to me to be raised by what he and some of those present had been saying. I wrote it as a letter to him, and asked him if he could allay my difficulty. He did not call for me to go and see him to discuss it, or write back to me, but at the start of his next lecture he had in his hand the pieces of paper on which I had written it, thanked me for raising the difficulty and discussed it brilliantly. Not long afterwards Alice Ambrose told me that he had spoken highly of my note and considered it worthy of publication, but I fear I did not do anything about that. I do not know whether I kept a copy of what I wrote, or whether Wittgenstein kept the piece or threw it away.[4]

---

[4] So I wrote when I made the first draft of this book. But, looking recently through some old papers I have accumulated over the years, I found a *rough* draft of the letter I wrote to Wittgenstein on that occasion. I have decided to include it in an Appendix, partly in case it had really something to it, and partly as an additional example of the sort of thing that was being discussed in those classes at the time (see p. 105).

5

Wittgenstein did not welcome people who attempted to come for a few sessions only. He called such people 'tourists', in contrast with serious students. I sympathised with his point of view on that matter, as the lectures normally took up what had been talked about the last time and anyone coming in and trying to latch on to the theme could easily have slowed up what he was trying to do, either through not making head or tail of what was being said, or by asking questions or making suggestions which had already been dealt with in previous lectures, or by disturbing his intense effort of thinking.

Wittgenstein could, however, also be pretty tough with the 'regulars' on matters of protocol. He was strictly punctual in starting each lecture. Now, on one occasion about that time, two of the class came in ten minutes late. Wittgenstein motioned to them impatiently to sit down in two deckchairs in the front which happened to be vacant, and then pulled out his watch from his breast pocket by the leather strap fastened to the buttonhole and, seeing the time, burst out, in a tone of great annoyance but also firm determination: 'When I *say* five o'clock, I *mean* five o'clock, and *not* ten-past-five. If you would prefer us to make it a quarter-past-five, it shall be a quarter-past-five, but then, please, a quarter-past-five, and *not twenty-past-five!*' Towards the end of this tirade his voice had gathered pace and force, and as he uttered the last few words he seemed as if he was administering a *coup-de-grâce* to some cowed animal.

6

During all the years I knew Wittgenstein his closest friend and disciple in Cambridge was Francis Skinner, a young Trinity man who had graduated brilliantly in mathematics, and had become deeply interested in philosophy. He had had osteomyelitis when a teenager and had a very bad limp. He wore special shoes with a high block-heel on his left shoe. He was not only a regular attendant at Wittgenstein's lectures but also personally devoted to Wittgenstein in an utterly unselfish and disinterested way. He was a very gentle person. He was tall and dark, with fine, closely-set, rather sad, brown eyes and a long, straightish nose. With his high forehead, he had a striking profile, which I sometimes thought would have looked admirable on a coin or medal. He had a pleasant, quiet, rather shy humour and a very kind disposition. He was slow of speech and diffident in expressing his opinions (though he often had quite strong ones). He did all sorts of practical chores for Wittgenstein and had long talks with him, and they often had meals together. He also on occasion made very intelligent contributions to the discussions in Wittgenstein's lectures and at the Moral Science Club. I imagine that discussion with Francis also could well have been of considerable value to Wittgenstein, so that the benefit in that respect was probably far from one-sided. I always liked and admired Francis, who was close to Wittgenstein in an apparently unambivalent way, which I could never have emulated myself. He was so strongly attached to Wittgenstein that, as I learned later, his parents felt outraged at what they considered to be the ruin of a promising career, and they were, I gathered, deeply hurt at the neglect of them which his concentrated friendship with Wittgenstein involved. I had a hint of this friction at one point which I shall mention shortly, but I would not have wanted to discuss it with Francis or with Wittgenstein, and I am quite unaware whether Francis felt at times badly under stress from the situation; but to me he never showed any outward signs of dissatisfaction with the choice he had made of becoming the valued and unsparing friend of a genius.

The hint of friction I mentioned just now came to the surface in a short episode revealing the rival claims. This occurred somewhat later when Wittgenstein was unwell in the College sick bay with a stone in his gall bladder and needed Francis particularly to be at hand in Cambridge at a weekend when his parents had expected him to go home for those days. Wittgenstein was baffled as to what could be done, and he asked my advice. I suggested that the best thing would be for Francis to telegraph his parents that he would come home for that weekend, but that if Wittgenstein was in dire need of him when the time came he should telegraph again at the last moment to put off the visit. Wittgenstein was delighted with my advice, and I remember distinctly the words in which he expressed his gratitude for it: 'Thank you for that lie!'

Much as I admired and liked Francis Skinner, I often felt over the years a welcome sense of escape and relief from the intensity of Wittgenstein's dominating personality in talking to more independent admirers of his such as Alice Ambrose, George Paul, Charles Hardie and Owen Storer, and later Margaret Ramsey and Richard Bosanquet. I also had friends who were quite unconnected with Wittgenstein and his philosophy. Moreover I sometimes went to other lectures in the Faculty of Moral Sciences – Moore's, Broad's, Ewing's, Braithwaite's, and

Wisdom's – and to Moore's tea-time At Homes in Chesterton Road.

.

7

In the summer of 1935 Wittgenstein and Francis Skinner invited me to have supper with them at Francis Skinner's lodgings above the Barbrooks' greengrocery shop at 81 East Road. When I arrived there I went upstairs and was welcomed by Wittgenstein who was sitting in a room with wooden boxes for seats, and a big box for a table. Francis was cooking a beef stew in the kitchen. Meanwhile Wittgenstein and I had a short chat, during which he said he wished I would teach Francis how to tell a story. (He seemed to think I was quite good at that.) When Francis emerged from the kitchen with the stewpot, he served us all with a great ladle. One forgot about the lack of creature comforts as the conversation moved into gear.

They talked about going to Russia together. They had both been learning Russian. They wanted to see what society was really like under the Communist system, and they planned to go there on a visit in September 1935. Like a fair number of people in England at that time they were more sympathetic to Communist Russia than to Nazi Germany or Fascist Italy. Francis, as one might have expected, was enthusiastic about the visit, and optimistic about where it might lead to for Wittgenstein and himself, though fairly indefinite as to quite what would come of it. Wittgenstein was soberer and more concrete in his prognosis. He was in the course of obtaining introductions that might help him to find suitable work in Russia if he were to decide to settle there, but he didn't seem at all sanguine as to his chances of getting some work there, even if as a result of the September visit he found he really wanted to.

After we finished our meal the conversation ran on the Russian language and Russian literature. They had both been greatly enjoying their Russian lessons and were keen on making substantial progress. Francis was by then working in The Cambridge Instrument Company but evidently spent a good deal of time on his Russian. Wittgenstein was intent on being able to read Tolstoy and Dostoyevsky in the original, and Francis had recently been reading some poems of Pushkin. They were both enchanted with the *sound* of the Russian language.[5]

Francis had a book of Russian poems in the room, and I asked him to show me one or two in the Russian text. I didn't know the Cyrillic alphabet at that time and was curious to know what the Russian texts of the poems actually looked like. I also felt I wanted to show interest in what Francis was intent on doing. So Francis showed me a few texts, and I then asked him to tell me the drift of some particular poem he had been struck by. He turned to a poem addressed to some men who had been condemned to work in Siberian mines. Wittgenstein chipped in at that point and asked me if I knew about the Decembrists. I had vaguely heard of them, but in 1935 I had made hardly any contact with the history of Russia and I had not even read *War and Peace*. So Wittgenstein explained who they were and why that poem was concerned with them. Some of them had been exiled to

---

[5] Their enthusiasm for the language, and for the Russian writers they mentioned, roused my own interest, and almost certainly helped to stir me to make a quite stout effort to learn Russian, and eventually to spend a good deal of several years later in life reading Tolstoy, and some other Russian novelists, mainly in English or French, but partly in Russian.

Siberia after a palace revolution in St Petersburg in 1825 and condemned to work in the mines. This poem, Francis then explained, was a message to those exiles. I asked him what the message was, and he said it was an encouragement to hold out proudly and patiently in their terrible situation and to realise that one day all would come right for them. As I stood by him he pointed to the poem, stanza by stanza, and gave me the gist of it. I cannot recall the actual words he used as he worked through it for me, so I give a literal translation in the note below.[6] He said that the account he gave could not of course match the power of the poem in Russian. Thereupon I asked him if he would be willing to read it for me in Russian, and he kindly agreed to do so. Now, however, as I search my memory, I cannot clearly decide whether or not he did read it to me. As I try to grasp that moment I feel unable to tell whether the succinct and powerful Russian stanzas of Pushkin which I hear in my mind's ear were actually read to me by Francis in his gentle but firm voice, or whether his reading is the child of my imagination.

[6] 'In the depth of the Siberian mines, persist in proud endurance; never shall perish your mournful labour, and the high aspiration of your souls.

'Hope, true sister of calamity, will, in the subterranean dark, awaken cheerfulness and mirth. The time one yearns for will arrive.

'Love and friendship will come to you through your dismal prison bars, just as my voice of freedom reaches you in your caves of servitude.

'Your heavy manacles will fall off, your dungeon walls will tumble down, and liberty will joyfully salute you at the gate, and brothers give you back your swords.'

8

I would not wish to evade mention of an important issue raised by the well-known fact that Wittgenstein had a number of close relationships with younger men, some of whom were also disciples. In some cases the men were also good-looking, and their appearance probably evoked aesthetic appreciation on Wittgenstein's part. The case I was most acquainted with was his close friendship with Francis Skinner, who has sometimes been referred to by writers on Wittgenstein as 'the Friend'. That term seems to me on the whole by no means unapt. It reminds one of the relationship between the poet and the young man in the first 126 of Shakespeare's Sonnets, where the poet's satisfaction, though involving a strong aesthetic element, is highly sublimated and sharply contrasted with his physical involvement with the Dark Woman. I am not suggesting, however, that the courtly and proud young man in the *Sonnets* resembled the modest and unostentatious Francis, nor that the friendship with Francis involved on Wittgenstein's part an obsessive infatuation comparable to that of the poet for the Friend in the *Sonnets*. In so far as I could sense its currents, the friendship of Wittgenstein and Francis seemed to me to include great, though physically undemonstrative, affection, high-level intellectual interchange and immense mutual respect, which nevertheless did not occlude light banter, or even serious criticism, at least on Wittgenstein's part. There was also a strong element of protection and care in Wittgenstein's attitude. I would be most sceptical of any suggestion that the friendship involved anything more lurid.

9

During the academical year 1935-6 another episode occurred which illustrated Wittgenstein's irritability. There was a rather gifted man, a graduate mathematician or engineer, from Peterhouse, as far as I can remember, who wanted to come to the lectures and took the precaution of asking Wittgenstein whether he might be allowed to do so. Now, before I started going to Wittgenstein's lectures, Francis Skinner, Margaret Masterman, Alice Ambrose and one or two others had actually taken down some of the important things Wittgenstein had been saying, and this material had been circulated to a few people, with Wittgenstein's approval, as *The Blue Book*. This Peterhouse (?) graduate knew shorthand, and he asked Wittgenstein if he might take down in shorthand what was said and, after Wittgenstein had vetted it, have it circulated to whomever Wittgenstein thought fit. Apparently Wittgenstein agreed to this, and H—— came a couple of times or so and took the proceedings down in shorthand and then typed them out. Unfortunately, I gather, he badly misjudged Wittgenstein's reaction to the typescript. Apparently he thought that Wittgenstein was so honest that he would want everything he said to appear in the draft submitted to him, and so the typescript included a good sprinkling of the oaths of which Wittgenstein characteristically delivered himself when he lost the thread of his thought or felt baffled and unable to proceed. H—— never appeared again, and I heard that Wittgenstein had been wild with anger and submitted the delinquent to a far from gentle dressing-down. This seemed to me more than a trifle harsh.

One thing Wittgenstein made amply clear was that he was far from keen that his work in progress should be circulated indiscriminately. He was not simply resentful that his ideas should be borrowed. He considered that they had often been misrepresented and garbled. He was also fiercely sensitive to the debased styles of some of the imitations. He cared fanatically about style. The impressive styles both of the hieratic *Tractatus* and of the more intimate *Philosophical Investigations* are indeed clearly an integral element in his philosophical achievement, and even part of the very essence of his modes of thought.

Nevertheless, despite his caution about circulation, Wittgenstein did allow a certain limited distribution of work which he did not yet consider ready for publication in print. Alice Ambrose had made several typescripts of what is now known as *The Brown Book*, and after she returned to the USA in 1935 she wrote to ask Wittgenstein to whom she might be allowed by him to send them. She had, I remember, mentioned to him several people as possible recipients. Wittgenstein then told me about this, and said that he had written to Alice to say that he would positively *like* her to send one to Moore and that he *would not mind* if she were to send one to me. She kindly sent me my copy in the spring of 1936. The result is that I still have, and treasure, that copy. I must confess, though, that from time to time I feel tempted to put into action a broad hint allegedly dropped by Wittgenstein at the end of a letter to someone: 'This signature is worth a hundred pounds!' If that story is true,[7] the boast was probably a mixture of mock bravado with a realisation that he was already famous and might in course of time even acquire the

---

[7] I have just heard from Alice Ambrose (Lazerowitz) that the story *is* true, and that she herself was the recipient of the letter.

commercial value to which he attached so little importance. If so, the declaration was shaded with an irony that would have had a characteristic appeal for Wittgenstein.

10

During the academical year October 1935 to June 1936 I got to know Wittgenstein much better personally. He asked me to tea with him in Trinity from time to time, and we ate supper at what he called 'Messrs Lyons and Co.' in Petty Cury. I also sometimes asked him back to tea or a frugal lunch at my lodgings in Bateman Street, and we occasionally went for a walk. We used to talk about all kinds of things: music, literature, people we knew, and people we only knew from books, or people whom he knew but I had not known, such as Frank Ramsey, for whose intelligence and character he had a strong admiration. (I remember Wittgenstein giving an example of Ramsey's acuteness. Ramsey went to visit Wittgenstein at a country school in Austria where he was for a time in the early 1920s teaching mathematics and various other subjects. Apparently in one of the classrooms there were several physiological diagrams posted on the walls, and one of them was designed to show how certain 'bad habits' could give one an enlarged heart. Ramsey evidently at once made the point that a pupil's ambition might well actually be to have as big a heart as he could.)

I can well remember a visit Wittgenstein paid to me at Bateman Street quite early on in that academical year 1935-36. I had a few hundred books in my rooms there. Among them was one called *Rudolf Eucken: his life and work.*[8] I had picked it up somewhere in London at a second-hand bookshop a few years earlier, rather naïvely, on the strength of a favourable remark in some book which I have altogether forgotten. The writer had spoken of 'Rudolf Eucken and Professor Otto' as deeply religious teachers, concerned with the immortality of the soul, which preoccupied me a good deal in my early twenties, when I had a great fear of annihilation but found it very hard to be convinced that anything else awaited us after the death of our bodies. Wittgenstein crouched down in front of my bookcases, looking at some of the books on the lower shelves and, picking out this unfortunate tome, asked me 'what on earth' I wanted to have *'that thing'* in my library for. I can't remember what answer I made, but I was so struck by his contemptuous attitude to the wretched book, and to the man it was about, that I determined then and there never to bother to read it, and indeed I never have. The strength of the impact Wittgenstein's attitude made on me in this case did, however, make me begin to feel wary lest I should succumb to domination in cases where the right might well not be on his side.

I did feel, on the one hand, that Wittgenstein felt very warmly towards me at that time. I was not only *flattered* by his often taking my arm when we went for a walk, calling me 'old man' and even telling me that I was 'decent' or 'intelligent', but also felt considerable affection towards him. I also admired what seemed to me to be his real genius and believed (what was certainly true) that I could learn a great deal from him, not only about philosophy but about people and about life in general. On the other hand at times I felt considerable reluctance to

---

[8] Rudolf Eucken (1846-1926), a German Idealist philosopher, who was awarded a Nobel Prize in 1908.

giving in to radical changes of attitude, including a change to that of a proud and even contemptuous austerity, and also a sense that what I had till then considered harmless luxuries were utterly trivial and unworthy of attachment. Nevertheless I found myself doing precisely this, and I was not quite sure what to think about it – whether I was now being healthily strong-minded or wretchedly weak under the influence of a powerful personality.

A couple of examples may serve to bring home the situation. Not long before Christmas 1935 I had been up to London to see my parents, and on my way back I happened to see on the station platform at Cambridge a Professor in the University who had been very kind to me and of whom I was very fond. He was bending down on the platform, and at first, from behind, I thought he was ill; but it turned out that he was only picking up the remains of some shattered bottles of fruit preserved in possibly alcoholic syrup. Now, under the influence of Wittgenstein, or at least of what I took to be his influence, I had come to think of such luxuries with a rather acrid kind of contempt. Therefore, although I helped the Professor pick up the pieces of broken glass and the syrupy fruit mixed in with it and deposit it all wrapped in some thick newspaper in a rubbish basket, my feelings of affection for him, and my sympathy for his disappointment at the shattering of the agreeable Christmas fare which he had brought home largely to please his family of young children, were curiously mingled with this other feeling of contempt, and even sorrow, that he had got his values all wrong. I was utterly convinced of that – though, I may perhaps add, I would be far from convinced of it now.

Another, somewhat similar, case occurred in the early summer of 1936. Graham Hough, Leo Salingar and I were chosen to represent the Cambridge University English Club in a debate at Oxford against the Oxford English Club on the motion 'The modern poet should write for the million'. I was housed in Magdalen by a rather conventional but moderately amiable young man whose name I have forgotten. He had arranged for me to spend the night in some rooms overlooking the gardens. When I arrived in the late afternoon I looked out of the bedroom window and saw a number of young men and women dressed in graceful and colourful costumes dancing what seemed to be elaborate figures of Elizabethan or Jacobean court dances. So narrow had my outlook become that I saw no beauty whatever in all this. It seemed wholly artificial and out of touch with the grim realities of what I had either heard or was to hear Wittgenstein refer to as 'civilisation, or whatever you call the bloody thing'. They seemed to be taking part in and enjoying something which appeared to me, as I looked at it, to be utterly frivolous and empty.

That these narrow convictions were not simply connected as figments of my imagination with Wittgenstein's own attitudes will probably be clear enough to anyone who knew him at the time, but it may be worth my mentioning a particular case in which Wittgenstein quite definitely and intentionally communicated to me his attitude on a fundamental matter. I used to go quite often to what was then called the Cosmopolitan Cinema ('the Cosmo', for short), which later became the Arts Cinema, and was ably managed by Norman Higgins. Well-chosen films, both British and foreign, were shown there. One evening I saw an English film in which Ralph Richardson took the part of a landowner, who seemed to me a thoroughly decent sort of chap, but who was morally condemned by the film, apparently simply for being a landowner. This struck me as grossly unfair, and not long afterwards I happened to tell Wittgenstein what I thought. His reply struck me, as so much of what he said used to do. He said that simply being a landowner could have been quite bad enough. I was not wholly convinced by that, but I was interested to find him saying something so clear-cut, despite the fact that he did not, as far as I knew, have any political affiliations at the time.

Wittgenstein's dislike of superficial fashion and worldly vanities had come out in another way in the spring of 1936. My mother and I were intending to spend our summer holiday in 1936 in Austria, Hungary and Czechoslovakia, and we were asking friends for advice as to where to stay in Austria. Someone had suggested to us Bad Ischl (a fashionable spa), but when I asked Wittgenstein his opinion, he turned the place down flat, suggesting instead Hallein, where, he added, an uncle of his used to have a castle.[9] This additional piece of information was also to some degree characteristic of Wittgenstein. He hated meretricious ostenstation and cultivated a severe simplicity, but he was also a scion of a wealthy upper-class Austrian family, and he sometimes surprised one by making this quite plain, as for instance in his frequent use of the term 'Ringstrasse' for things he considered to be second-rate. I gathered from friends that he had at one time been attracted politically by the Austrian Nationalist movement, in which Major Fey had taken a leading part, but had later become disillusioned with it. In the end my mother and I went neither to Bad

[9] I had not the slightest inkling at that time of the deep significance that Hallein and his uncle Paul's castle had had for Wittgenstein, shortly after World War I, when Wittgenstein was feeling suicidal, and his uncle invited him to stay at his castle for a time, with the result that Wittgenstein was enabled to emerge from that bout of depression, and to immerse himself in constructive philosophical work again (see Brian McGuinness, *Wittgenstein, A Life: Young Ludwig 1889-1921*, London 1988, p. 264.)

Ischl nor to Hallein. I am not quite sure why. In Austria we spent most of our time in the Tyrol at Innsbruck and at Igls in the hills nearby, though we did spend a few days in Vienna before going on to Hungary and Czechoslovakia.

11

I generally enjoyed Wittgenstein's company for part of the time I was with him, but I often felt a sense of oppression, especially indoors. Simply being in the same room with him was far from comfortable. I was especially irritated when, as happened on more than one occasion, he called to see me, sat down, without a word, in an easy chair, tilted his head back and half-closed his eyes, apparently lost in thought and quite silent, and eventually came out with some remark which seemed to be getting at one didactically in a direct or indirect way. I even suspected his preliminary silences (probably quite unjustifiably) as a form of affectation, or even as an intentional form of hypnotism, and I resented it on either count. One particular result of this was rather curious. He had suddenly suggested that one morning I should go to his rooms in Whewell's Court, and take down some philosophical thoughts which he might dictate. This seemed to me a very worthwhile thing to do, but when the morning came round I did not feel that I could stand any of those possible long silences, so I took with me a book which I was reading at the time, Condillac's *Traité des Systèmes*.[10] When I got to his rooms, armed with

[10] Étienne Bonnot, Abbé de Condillac (1714-1780), philosopher and economist. In his *Traité des Systèmes* (1749), he has penetrating

paper, he welcomed me in and then sat down in a deck chair, tilted his head back, half-closed his eyes, and remained for an appreciable time completely silent. I found this too oppressive, and so I picked up the Condillac and started to read it. Wittgenstein still sat with eyes closed, and said nothing, and his silence allowed me to read several pages of that fascinating book, which, indeed, was far from irrelevant to the sort of philosophy which he himself was practising in relation to metaphysical systems. After a while he suddenly opened his eyes wide, and asked: 'What's that you're reading?' I told him, and he asked to have a look at the book. I had expected he would be annoyed at my reading it instead of simply waiting for him to start dictating to me, but he was either not annoyed or else disguised his annoyance with some subtlety. He read a few pages of the book, and I asked him what he thought of them. 'Not bad', was his answer, and that, in his vocabulary, was pretty laudatory. He then said, however, that he did not really feel like dictating anything that morning, and suggested going for a walk instead. This we did, but the idea of dictating things to me was not mentioned again till some time later.

Not long after the Condillac episode I can remember his inviting me to tea in his rooms, and providing marzipan potatoes as the cakes. I had always been partial to them, though he did not know this. There were three potatoes on a plate, and after I had eaten one he offered me another. He himself just drank tea. I took a second potato; but, in order not to give the impression of self-indulgence to someone I reckoned to be austere

---

criticisms of the metaphysical systems of Descartes, Malebranche, Leibniz and Spinoza. His critiques include detailed indications of the imaginative exaggerations and linguistic indeterminacy of key concepts of the system concerned.

about eating, I left a small piece on my plate. I *may* also have intended that as a sign that I didn't want the third potato, but I'm not sure. At all events, his comment was unambiguous: 'I say, what an affectation!' But he didn't say it very seriously, and the rest of our time passed in pleasant conversation. Before he put the tea things away, however, I was much struck by his getting out a pan and brush and sweeping the crumbs from the corded carpet. I don't know how much this was simply to save them being trodden in, and how much deliberately to save the bedmaker work; but I think, in retrospect, that the latter point had some weight. It would have chimed with the deep Tolstoyan influence on him, about which I only came to know much later.

Either on this occasion or somewhat later, he asked me if I would like to see his bedroom. I couldn't imagine why he wanted to show it to me, but I was certainly impressed by its simplicity, neatness and cleanliness. There was something monastic (or possibly military – possibly, indeed, both) about the atmosphere. He had also in the bedroom, however, a small bookcase full of books. I can remember seeing among them works of Novalis and of Keller, and also Goethe's *Faust*. He remarked on the books not being philosophical and said: 'I wonder what people would think. He calls himself a philosopher, but he has no philosophical books!' There was an element of pride in this, and also something suggesting the *panache* of a conjurer, or French cook, who reputedly makes something out of nothing. I asked him whether he had read Goethe's *Faust* recently (I had been doing so myself), and he replied that he hadn't, as he 'hadn't needed it'. He did, however, add the useful opinion that he thought that Bayard Taylor's English translation (which I actually possessed in the World's Classics) represented the spirit of *Faust* extremely well.

Although Wittgenstein had no philosophical books in that small library, it was clear to me that he had read a fair amount of philosophy at one time or another. He seemed to have read a reasonable amount of Plato, for instance, Augustine's *Confessions* and also some of Kant, Schopenhauer and Nietzsche. Among more modern writers he had read some of Frege, Russell and Moore, besides of course taking part in sessions of the Vienna Circle. The piece he admired most of Moore's was the essay 'A Defence of Common Sense'. He said he thought Whitehead had considerable mathematical, but not much philosophical, talent. Russell, on the other hand, he considered to have high philosophical talent but little quality as a writer. He said that he could not remember a single *sentence* that Russell ever wrote. When I asked him what philosopher he thought *did* write impressively his immediate reply was 'Nietzsche'. Now, I happened to have read a certain amount both of Schopenhauer and of Nietzsche by that time. I had been stimulated to do so some years earlier by my friend Cuthbert Scott of King's.[11] I was therefore interested by Wittgenstein's opinions of their work. Of Schopenhauer I can remember him once saying to me 'Well, he *was* a philosopher', and, when I asked him what he meant by a 'philosopher', unexpectedly replying, 'A teacher of manners.' I have indeed become progressively more and more convinced that Wittgenstein thought that it was far more important to be a teacher of 'manners', in the sense of *morals*, than to be an ingenious logician or brilliant scientist.

When I told him I had read a certain amount of

[11] J.M.C. Scott, later known as 'John Scott'. He was a distinguished Applied Mathematician, and eventually, after a time at Harwell, lectured in Applied Mathematics at Cambridge, where he was a Fellow of Selwyn till he died in 1974 on a hill-walking holiday with his wife in Switzerland.

Nietzsche and asked what he thought of his general world view, he said that he didn't think there was much 'consolation' to be had from it – it was 'too shallow'. Hegel he said he had read hardly at all, but from what he *had* read he thought Hegel 'had nose' – he was struck, for instance, by Hegel's denial of the so-called 'law of contradiction'. That denial, indeed, could well have appealed to Wittgenstein's love of paradox, which came out from time to time on various occasions. One instance I remember was a reference he made in a lecture to a fairy story in which a hero had to perform various apparently impossible tasks for an exacting monarch who threatened him with death in case of failure but promised him a great reward in case of success. One task was to bring a certain beautiful girl to the King's court 'neither naked nor dressed'. The hero took some time to come to the right solution, but eventually tumbled to it, and produced the damsel wearing a net garment. Wittgenstein was clearly delighted both by the paradox and by its solution.

12

Wittgenstein was a fervent film addict. He used to go a great deal to see American wild-west and gangster films at the Kinema in Mill Road. At some stage of our acquaintance he told me that he didn't know how he could have done without them. He used also to read tough stories in such periodicals as *The Red Magazine*. This sort of fare clearly corresponded to some deep need in Wittgenstein's character; but I never came to understand quite how that worked. On the other hand he recognized the strength of 'needs' in other people to see

films, or read books or magazines, and a 'need' was
evidently an important criterion of genuineness in his
way of looking at things. I can remember his delight on
one occasion when I was walking along Trinity Street
with him, and a stranger, who evidently didn't know
Cambridge, asked us if there was 'a cinema near 'andy'.
When the man had been told by us that there was one in
Market Hill, just round the corner, and gone off in great
glee, Wittgenstein repeated the phrase 'near 'andy' with
relish.

Wittgenstein had apparently no similar need for music
of a kind which could reasonably be considered analogous
to what he consumed in the form of films and tough
stories. On the other hand he did approve of light popular
music as a background to shopping in such emporia as
Woolworth's. But he never gave it the concentrated
attention that he apparently gave the rough films and
magazine stories.

13

Wittgenstein said to me on more than one occasion: 'The
trouble with you and me, old man, is that we have no
religion!' I don't think I ever plumbed the full depth of
this statement, either as applied to himself or as applied
to me, though I think I have a somewhat better insight
into his meaning now than I ever did in those days. As far
as he was concerned, I can remember that more than
once on going to his rooms for a talk or for tea I found him
reading the Bible. One day he said he thought it would be
a good thing if we would read the Book of Job together.
We never did, but I think I now understand why it might
have been good for both of us. We were certainly both

impatient people, and I still am. Wittgenstein also once took me along one afternoon to Little St Mary's Church, a very 'High' Church, which he was much attached to, though I dó not know whether he ever attended any services there. He simply took me into the church and we sat down in a pew near the back, on the south side, and just continued to sit there in silence. While we were sitting there a middle-aged woman came into the church, went into one of the pews about halfway up on the north side, and knelt down to pray. Wittgenstein leant over to me and whispered: *'That* is what a church is for!'

Another place he took me to, when I was still lodging in Bateman Street, was the Botanic Garden. This I already knew reasonably well in a superficial way, but a stroll round it with Wittgenstein had a character of its own. He especially liked the interior of the glasshouses, and breathed in the odour of the aromatic plants with undisguised, perhaps even with ostentatious, delight. I can remember his saying how fine he thought the Botanic Garden was, and also, very characteristically, that he thought that gardeners did not receive the honour they deserved.[12]

14

In the early summer of 1936 I was having tea with Wittgenstein in his rooms in Whewell's Court, the day after some great party in the Court had been held by undergraduates and graduate students. There had been fireworks, and also some actual minor conflagration.

[12] I had no idea at that time that he had worked as a gardener's assistant in a monastery near Vienna (in 1926 shortly after he gave up schoolmastering).

When we were having tea there was a knock on the door, and a porter came in to deliver some letters for Wittgenstein. The porter said that he hoped that Wittgenstein had not been disturbed by the party the night before. Wittgenstein said he thought the fireworks had been a good thing. This seemed to shock the porter, and he said that something had been set on fire. 'Good!' said Wittgenstein, which the porter clearly considered a somewhat eccentric comment, and accordingly rejoined that he was afraid they might damage the ' 'Ermes'. 'That's just what I hoped they would do!' was Wittgenstein's final riposte. He had long had the greatest contempt for that *objet d'art*, a bronze figure in what he considered a pretentiously pensive posture as if it were able to think thoughts of any value. After Wittgenstein had expressed his strange attitude, the porter retired in evident perplexity.

15

Although I believe that the vast majority of the episodes and remarks I have so far mentioned occurred before August 1936, I am somewhat uncertain whether they *all* did. In any case I left after July 1936 for a period of continental travel, from which I did not return to Cambridge until October 1937. Wittgenstein was also away from Cambridge for much of that time. He had thought of settling in Russia, and had visited Moscow and Leningrad in September 1935. He and Francis Skinner had had Russian lessons in 1934 from Fanya Pascal, the Russian wife of Roy Pascal, a distinguished

Germanist, at that time a University Lecturer at Cambridge and a Fellow of Pembroke College.[13] Wittgenstein went to Fanya Pascal again, alone, for Russian conversation in 1935, before his Russian visit. He abandoned the plan to settle there, and returned to Cambridge, where he remained till the summer of 1936, when he went on a short holiday to France, and then to his hut in Norway, where he remained till the end of 1936. He came to Cambridge for a week or so in January 1937 and then went back to Norway, eventually returning to Cambridge towards the end of 1937.

Wittgenstein's lectures did not start again until the Lent Term 1938. I had myself been elected to a Research Studentship in Philosophy in October 1937 at St John's. During the Michaelmas Term 1937 I attended the Moral Science Club meetings pretty regularly. There was a great interest in the topic of 'Simples', the simple elements, e.g. sense-data, out of which the physical world could be regarded as constructed. Four meetings were devoted to that subject.

In January 1938 I had only just returned for the Full Lent Term when I received a postcard from J.C. Taylor, an Australian undergraduate then in his final year at Trinity, telling me that Wittgenstein had started lecturing that week, but didn't want too many people to come, and so the lectures were not 'open lectures', but for people Wittgenstein had 'decided on' to attend if they wished, one of whom was 'naturally' me, so, in case I would care to come Taylor said the next lecture would be on the following day at 2 pm in Taylor's rooms (K2,

---

[13] Roy Pascal later became Professor of German at the University of Birmingham. His wife Fanya contributed a fascinating personal memoir of Wittgenstein to the volume edited by Rush Rhees called *Ludwig Wittgenstein: Personal Recollections*, Oxford 1981.

Whewell's Court)[14] and would last till 4.30 or 5. The lectures were to be twice a week for two hours each. Of course I went, and I continued to do so throughout the academical year. There were ten or twelve of us there, and it was concentrated hard work for most of us. I noticed, however, that one of the class wore very large horn-rimmed dark glasses behind which he could have at least relaxed (or even perhaps slept) had he found the intellectual tension too taxing. The lectures were about the foundations of mathematics.

I am somewhat hazy about who were at the lectures in those Lent and Easter Terms 1938 but, apart from Taylor and myself, I believe the group included Francis Skinner, George Paul, Rush Rhees, Yorick Smythies, Francis Kitto, Alister Watson, Casimir Lewy and Douglas Gasking.[15] I am not sure whether Richard Bosanquet was already there or whether he did not come till the Michaelmas Term. Nor am I sure whether Margaret Ramsey was there. (She became Margaret Paul that spring). The lectures were held in rooms of various pupils of Wittgenstein, including Taylor and Rhees.

From the autumn of 1937 I had been lodging at The Hermitage in Silver Street, at that time a guest-house under the characterful direction of Miss Cragoe, an elderly but energetic and resourceful Cornish lady nicknamed 'The Crag', though that appellation didn't do justice to her pleasantness and tact. Early in 1938, after I had been attending Wittgenstein's lectures for a while, he called on me there. I was fortunate enough to be

[14] Wittgenstein's Fellowship had expired in 1936, and he no longer occupied his old rooms.

[15] Gasking and A.C. Jackson wrote a short article on Wittgenstein as a teacher, in *The Australasian Journal of Philosophy 29*, No. 2 (1951). It is reprinted in *Ludwig Wittgenstein: The Man and his Philosophy*, a collection of essays by various writers, ed. K.T. Fann, New Jersey & Hassocks, 1978.

installed in a delightful room at the back of the house, overlooking a small tributary of the river. The room eventually became that of Dr Rosemary Murray when she was President of New Hall. When Wittgenstein caught sight of the view from the window he could not contain himself but burst out excitedly: 'Well, old man, you *are* an aesthete!'

At that time I had for some years been suffering intermittently with sinusitis. Sometimes it was the maxillary sinuses, but that year it was the frontal sinuses. At times it was very painful and at others at least impaired my concentration. Wittgenstein was very concerned about this and actually bought me a small hot-water bottle which he recommended me to put on my forehead to try to drain the mucus away. He also told me that he had found it beneficial when he was having difficulty in doing concentrated work to take 'acid sodium phosphate'[16] (NaH_2PO_4), which he advised me to buy in pure crystalline form. He made a point of helping his friends in this way and even regarded it as a *criterion* of friendship to do so. It was likewise a point of honour with him to visit a friend if he were ill. One should do that sort of thing, of course; but Wittgenstein was more than usually punctilious about it. Another matter on which he was equally punctilious was his horror of keeping anyone waiting for any appointment he had made. I remember going with him on an afternoon walk past the gasworks and as we were returning his suddenly remembering that he had arranged to meet someone in Cambridge about a quarter of an hour before. He was extremely agitated and rushed with me up to the Newmarket Road, in the hope of hailing a taxi. That hope seemed to me fairly forlorn; but, as luck would have it, in less than a

[16]Generally English chemists call it 'sodium acid phosphate'.

minute an empty taxi appeared, making for the town. We both hailed it and got in. Wittgenstein was *enormously* relieved. When we were nearing the middle of the town he asked me in a low voice, in very well pronounced French: 'Combien est-ce qu'on lui donne?' That seemed to me interesting. The question appeared to reveal both an ignorance of the going rate of tips and also perhaps a certain delicacy about letting the driver know what the problem was.

16

It was some time before I came to know of Wittgenstein's admiration of Napoleon, and his apparently incongruous admiration for Tolstoy, who was so deeply critical of Napoleon. I distinctly remember that this came out during a long walk I had with him along the north bank of the Cam in the direction of Horningsea. What he admired in Napoleon was his energy and resourcefulness, and, in particular, his capacity to switch his concentration rapidly from some enterprise that did not promise success, such as his projected invasion of England in 1804, to some operation that seemed distinctly more auspicious, such as a drive to the East. Wittgenstein strongly recommended me to read Général de Ségur's *Mémoires d'un Aide-de-Camp de Napoléon*, and I bought a copy shortly afterwards. I also bought Ségur's *La Campagne de Russie*. I had no idea at the time, however, what a special interest those books must have had for Wittgenstein who had served in the Austrian army on the Russian front in World War I. He had, though, a profounder admiration for Tolstoy than for Napoleon. He had obviously read *War and Peace* and been deeply impressed by the sharply critical attitude towards Napoleon embodied in that book. The opposition between Napoleon's worldly attitude to life and Tolstoy's religious fervency and austerity was indeed clearly very important to Wittgenstein. Yet I was wholly unaware how great a part Tolstoy's translation of the Gospels had played in Wittgenstein's life during the campaign on the Eastern front, and I only came to know years later how profoundly he admired Tolstoy's *Twenty-three Tales*. It was Piero Sraffa who told me in the 1960s that Wittgenstein had once given him a copy of those tales for a present. The figures of Napoleon and Tolstoy must indeed have bulked large in Wittgenstein's imagination over the years and taken on something of a symbolic character.

17

Among the novelists I remember Wittgenstein speaking of with enthusiasm were Sterne, Dickens, Tolstoy, Dostoyevsky and Gottfried Keller. He told me he had read *Tristram Shandy* about a dozen times. I don't know how Wittgenstein's admiration for Sterne originated. It *could* have been through his reading of Tolstoy, who was a strong admirer of both *Tristram Shandy* and *A Sentimental Journey*, but I have no idea when he first encountered Sterne's work. Unfortunately I have forgotten any specific things he may have said to me about Sterne, but I could understand something of the appeal *Tristram Shandy* could have had for him: such as the preposterous conception of the whole book, the freedom and surprise of the writing, the whimsicality, the engagingness and vividness of the characters and the nimble and subtle wit. A few days after telling me how much he enjoyed and admired *Tristram Shandy*, a rather droll result ensued. Wittgenstein may have been re-reading the novel. At all events he said to me that he had been struck with a passage in it which seemed to be a quotation from Aristotle which said that a man looks *up* when he is thinking of the *future* and *down* when he is thinking of the *past*. Crediting me with more learning than I possessed, but knowing that I had been reading quite a bit of Aristotle recently, he asked me if I could say which work of Aristotle it came from. I had no recollection whatever of any such passage. He said that the passage was quoted in *Tristram Shandy*[17] as from 'Aristotle's Masterpiece'. I said I was sorry, but I didn't know the answer. Then, a few days later, he told me not to bother to look any further in Aristotle as he had now heard that *Aristotle's Masterpiece* was a bawdy eighteenth-century book. This was *quite* near the mark, but only *quite*.

Aristotle's Master-Piece was actually a compendium including an eighteenth-century version of a manual of sex, a midwife's guide, a book of homely remedies and a miscellany of rustic science. It ran through many editions, and it had reached the twenty-seventh edition in 1759, just before Volumes I and II of *Tristram Shandy* appeared in 1760. However, the passage about looking down and looking up, which had struck Wittgenstein, was not from *Aristotle's Master-Piece* but from another work frequently bound up with it, *Aristotle's Book of Problems*. The twenty-fifth edition of this book was published in 1755 and bound up with the 1759 edition of

[17] *Tristram Shandy*, vol. 2 ch. 7: 'It is said in *Aristotle's Master-Piece*, "That when a man doth think of any thing which is past, – he looketh down upon the ground; – but that when he thinketh of something which is to come, he looketh up towards the heavens".' And, in the following paragraph the narrator reveals that 'My uncle *Toby*, I suppose, thought of neither, for he looked horizontally' – towards, by implication, the right or wrong end of Widow Wadman.

the *Master-Piece*. The *Problemata* was probably origin-
ally a Peripatetic work, possibly containing some
questions raised by Aristotle himself, but probably
compiled over a long period by various hands. The oldest
manuscript is tenth-century. In the 1755 edition of this
book there are two questions posed which are relevant to
the *Tristram Shandy* passage: (1) Why doth a Man lift up
his head towards the Heavens when he doth imagine?
(Not quite the same point as in *Tristram Shandy*), and
(2) Why doth a Man when he museth, or thinketh on
things past, look down towards the earth? (This *is*, of
course, the question that the *Tristram Shandy* passage
purports to answer.)

Wittgenstein could well have been both interested and
amused by the answers given in *Aristotle's Book of
Problems* to the two questions as there raised: (1)
'Because the Imagination is in the fore part of the Head,
or Brain, and therefore it lifteth up itself, that the Creeks
or Cells of the Imagination may be opened, and the
Spirits which help the Imagination, and are fit for that
purpose, having their concourse thither, may help the
Imagination'; and (2) 'Because the Cell or Creek which is
behind, is the Creek or Chamber of Memory, and
therefore that looketh towards Heaven when the head is
bowed down; and so that Cell is opened to the end that
the Spirits which perfect the Memory should enter in'
(*Aristotle's Book of Problems*, 1755 edition, pp. 9-10). This
sort of explanation, even if quite false, could well have
appealed to Wittgenstein's interest in physiology, and
also for its attempt, however quaint, to trace causal
connexions as an engineer might do.[18]

---

[18] For the whole matter see the edition of *Tristram Shandy*, ed.
Melvyn New, together with Richard A. Davies and W.G. Day, 3 vols.,
Gainsville, University of Florida Press, 1984, vol. 1 (text), p. 117 and
vol. 3 (notes), pp. 149-50.

As for Dickens, I can only actually recall his mentioning *A Christmas Carol*, though it seems that he had read various other Dickens novels, and we may even have discussed one or more of them. (I regret now that I didn't keep some kind of diary in which I could have made some brief notes of what he said about particular novels.) He certainly admired the spirit of *A Christmas Carol*.

Dostoyevsky *and* Tolstoy were, however, for him the greatest novelists. *Crime and Punishment* he told me he had read at least ten times, and both in that novel and in *The Brothers Karamazov* he thought Dostoyevsky expressed 'a whole religion'. All the same, Tolstoy appealed to him even more. He shared with Tolstoy the experience of serving in the Army in a big war, and also of spending his youth in a prosperous family. Toushine, a minor character in *War and Peace*, seemed to him especially admirable, serving selflessly and effectively as a Captain without any ostentation, a symbol of the best in the Russian resistance to Napoleon. The moral element in *War and Peace* was clearly of great importance for Wittgenstein. On the other hand he criticised both *War and Peace* and *Anna Karenina* for their sometimes bewildering transitions. But the range of life treated and the depth of insight revealed in these two great novels impressed him profoundly.

Gottfried Keller I didn't know at all, but Wittgenstein thought so highly of his novels and stories that I decided to try one at least, in English. So I borrowed a translation of *Kleider machen Leute* from the University Library. Although I had done a year's German at school I could read only slowly. I liked the story enough to want to read more Keller, and, if possible, in German some day. (When I got to know more German I actually read a number of Keller's stories, the *Sieben Legenden*, after the war, with an Austrian friend. We read them aloud in German alternately, and my friend immediately translated the German where I didn't understand it. I have been grateful to Wittgenstein for bringing Keller into my ken.)

18

It is well enough known that Wittgenstein came from a musical family, that his parents were friends of Brahms, that his pianist brother Paul Wittgenstein lost an arm in World War I and that Ravel wrote for Paul his celebrated Concerto for the Left Hand.

Wittgenstein himself had learned the clarinet at one time; but he told me that he had not really got very far with it and had concentrated largely on achieving a good tone. Yet, though he no longer played a musical instrument at the time I first met him in 1934, he had acquired considerable skill in whistling tunes. He clearly had a fine ear and also great sensitiveness to the sounds, feelings and moods of music. He was, moreover, deeply concerned with it and had both strong enthusiasms and high critical standards.

My recollection is that during the time I knew him the composers of whom he spoke most warmly were Mozart, Schubert and Brahms. About Beethoven I can well remember his saying: 'I've no doubt that anything the old man wrote was good, but it doesn't *mean* much to *me* – except for the symphonies.' I could not even get him to agree to listen to the wonderful slow movement of Beethoven's last String Quartet, Op. 135, which I had had from schooldays on an HMV 78 rpm gramophone record for which it had been played by the Flonzaley Quartet. I could not conceive of his having any difficulty in responding to that movement, but he obstinately refused to listen to it. In all fairness, however, it must be added that he may well have tried the whole work before and got nothing out of any of it.

Wittgenstein was not very keen on opera. He far preferred Lieder, and he told me more than once that he thought that singers who made their name in opera seldom managed to be good Lieder singers too.

As for modern conductors, the only one I ever heard him mention with deep respect was Toscanini.

Wittgenstein hated humbug, and he thought there was a good deal too much of it around in the modern musical world.

I have always been keen on playing piano duets, and I believe it was Wittgenstein who first put me on to Mozart's Original Compositions for Four Hands, which have given me great enjoyment over the years. I shared with him a particular enthusiasm for a subject in the second movement (Andante) of the F Major Sonata (K. 497), and we both whistled it with delight. He may also have been the first person to mention to me the Schubert Original Compositions for Four Hands, though I did not embark on any of these till much later.

Wittgenstein was certainly amazed at the creative power and versatility of Schubert. Among the compositions he thought most highly of was the C Major Quintet. He was astonished that quite late in Schubert's career he should have decided to take *lessons* in counterpoint!

As for Brahms's music, Wittgenstein naturally felt a special relation with it because of his parents' friendship with Brahms, who often went to their house in Vienna in the Alleegasse. I cannot help wondering indeed whether the fact that Brahms's Clarinet Quintet had been performed privately in the family house specially for Brahms to hear may have had some part in causing him eventually to learn the clarinet. This idea of mine is purely speculative. Yet it is certain that when he started as a schoolmaster in Austria after serving in World War I he was required, among other duties, to *teach* an instrument, and apparently he had not seriously learned any particular instrument already. He chose the clarinet. As for Brahms's music in general, he often expressed his admiration of it, and he contrasted it with that of Mendelssohn, which, in his view, only occasionally attained the generally high level of that of Brahms.

I shall now simply record a few scattered moments when I had personal contact with Wittgenstein in a musical context.

I start with one relating to Brahms whose music was a passion for Wittgenstein. I vividly remember walking with him one afternoon in the town. We were about to pass in front of the Great Gate of St John's College when we heard through an open window of the Music Room a passage from the Third Symphony (in F major). The passage was from the third movement, the *Poco allegretto*, in C minor. He stopped, and motioned to me to stop too. He seemed spellbound. As the wonderful lyrical crescendoes unfolded, he drew in his breath, and his facial expression responded to the music with striking sensitivity. We stood there for about a minute, I should say, till the short movement ended. He was radiant with enthusiasm and satisfaction.

A more amusing musical episode, trivial but significant, occurred one day when he was talking with me about Bizet. He evidently liked Bizet, and he told me that Bizet had appealed to Nietzsche as 'Southern music', in contrast with the 'Northern music' of Wagner. I had recently been playing to myself through a piano score of *L'Arlésienne* and had enjoyed the work keenly. I told him how much I had liked it, and he said he liked it too. I

asked him if he remembered the opening theme of the
Overture and started to hum it. He said I had not got it
quite right, and he tried to whistle it correctly, as he
thought. He was very proficient at whistling and sometimes whistled splendidly to piano accompaniment. This
time, though, he didn't get the melody right, and I had the
face to say so and tried to whistle it correctly myself. My
whistling was not as technically skilful as his, but this
time I am pretty sure that it was at least accurate. He was
annoyed and burst out: 'We *are* a couple of asses!' I fear I
continued to believe that I was not one of them, but I let
the matter drop. He didn't respond kindly to correction,
and he was also at times over-confident and even rash in
expressing opinions which turned out to be woefully wide
of the mark.[19] That over-confidence and rashness, however, were the counterpart of his characteristic merits of
energy and boldness.

From time to time in conversation he made illuminating (or at least thought-provoking) comments on the
general drift of a musical work or passage. I can recall
two which seemed to me particularly striking. One day I
had been listening to the Ninth Symphony of Beethoven
and he asked me what I considered the drift of it to be. I
said it seemed to me to represent a revolution. He agreed
with that, but with a modification: 'Yes, but an *ideal*
revolution.' On another occasion he happened to call on
me when I was practising the top part of Mozart's Fugue
in G Minor for Four Hands (K. 401). He asked me what I
imagined it to mean. I said I had no idea. 'Well,' he
replied, 'it's the eternity of the damned!' When I told a
great authority on Mozart's music of this comment, he

[19] For example, his dismissal of newspaper rumours in 1938 that
Hitler was about to invade Austria (see M.O'C. Drury's admirable
'Conversations with Wittgenstein' in *Ludwig Wittgenstein: Personal
Recollections*, ed. Rush Rhees, Oxford 1981, p. 153).

dismissed it with contempt as 'subjective stuff and nonsense!' No doubt, however, that was what the fugue meant to Wittgenstein's imagination. Yet it might well have been purely subjective. At certain moments in my own imagination he himself seemed to me to resemble my own image of Milton's Satan, but that could well be purely subjective too. It seems hard to determine the weight of such imaginative claims. Another time I had been exploring Schubert's *Die Winterreise*. I was fairly familiar with *Die schöne Müllerin* by then. I had sung those songs often in the family in my fashion, but not *Die Winterreise*. Wittgenstein happened to call in when I had got to the last song of the cycle: 'Der Leiermann.' Readers may remember that this is about an old organgrinder who stands at the end of a village monotonously turning the handle of his barrel-organ with his fingers stiff with cold and tottering barefooted on the ice. His collection plate is always empty. No one wants to hear him and no one notices him, and the dogs snarl round him. Yet he lets things happen as they may and goes on turning the handle, and his organ is never silent. The narrator bursts out in amazement at the old man: 'Funny old fellow, shall I go along with you? Do you want to roll out my songs on your organ?' Wittgenstein asked me to play the piano accompaniment. When I started off with a few bars he criticised my *tempo* for not being quite regular and monotonous enough. He was also insistent that the semiquaver rests should always be brought out clearly, and he was keen that the accentuated beats should suggest the mechanical hiccups (*my* word) of the hurdy-gurdy. We went through the whole accompaniment, and once it seemed to him in order he whistled the song part right through, admirably. As far as the text was concerned he wanted me to be aware of the monotony of the repetitions, and he also noted the balance of the realism of the happenings and the calm tolerance of the old man. The wistfulness of the ending did not seem to him sentimental but buoyant, and he threw in the comment that, though Schumann's music was sometimes sentimental, Schubert's *never* was.

It is probably worth adding here something Wittgenstein said to me about another Southern composer: Rossini. I had been enthralled by the energy of *The Barber of Seville*, and by some of the Overtures, and one day I asked Wittgenstein what he thought of Rossini. His comment was not negative, but deftly 'placing': 'Well, if you want a canary! ...'

This seems probably nearly enough for the time being about contacts with Wittgenstein in musical contexts. I shall mention one or two more later: but there is one quite lengthy episode involving music that I would like to recount here, and I devote the next section to it.

19

Wittgenstein's character was certainly not monotonous. His capacity to surprise was quite considerable. In May 1938 he suddenly asked me if I would like to go with him to the Festival Theatre to hear 'a very great artiste', Yvette Guilbert. I didn't know about her. He told me that she was a *diseuse*, and what that meant. I accepted his invitation with pleasure, and the whole performance was a delight.

Yvette Guilbert was about 71 at the time but her voice was still flexible, and her artistry was remarkable. The songs were varied in type, and covered a wide period, from the twelfth century to the early twentieth. The first Part of the programme consisted of six medieval songs.

The first two were narratives of Christ's Nativity and Passion. Then came two rebellious secular songs by women whose marriages were unhappy. Finally there were two adventures from the feudal period, one tragic and the other with a happy ending. The Nativity song was sixteenth-century. The simple colloquial words which narrated the tiring search for nearly six hours by Joseph and Mary, to find accommodation in Bethlehem, were charming, and the call of each hour by the night watchman was dramatic and gave firm structure to the song. The narrative of the Passion was fifteenth-century. It was less impressive, and geared rather crudely to the promise of indulgence to the hearers who will understand the Passion and publish it to the world. I cannot remember clearly how Wittgenstein reacted to the religious songs, but I recall vaguely that he preferred the first. He certainly relished both the secular songs. He enjoyed the piquancy of the protest by the unhappily married woman who complained at her husband beating her: 'Pourquoi me bat mon mari?' She never did him any wrong, or spoke badly of him. She only had 'un doux ami'. Wittgenstein also evidently appreciated the strength of the other song, in which the woman planned how to get rid of her husband. It was clear to me that he had a very good understanding of French and enjoyed the racy vigour of the woman's outburst. As to the feudal songs, they were both ballads. One was a version of the famous Renaud (Arnaud) story, and the other, happier one recounted a King's imprisonment of his daughter who refused to give up her intention of marrying the man she loved. She feigned death and was wrapped in a shroud, but her beloved, passing by, cut the threads and delivered her. Whereupon the King relented and the lovers were married. Unfortunately my memory is a complete blank as to how Wittgenstein responded to the two ballads. And then came the Interval.

During that interval, however, when we were discussing Yvette Guilbert and her performance, whose artistry Wittgenstein again praised very highly, he suddenly said to me: 'The trouble with you and me, old man, is that we are too civilised!' I thought I detected in this remark a certain ambivalence in his attitude to the whole occasion. I suspected that the occasion involved some element of a not altogether welcome throwback to his pre-World War I life, when he had even led a quite social existence with his brothers and sisters, and friends, and been considered as something of an 'aesthete'.[20] (In this respect, as in *some* others, the pattern of Wittgenstein's evolution resembled that of Tolstoy, who as a young man had shocked an admirer of his work by his dandyish appearance. Even very late in life Tolstoy's own attitudes were notably ambivalent, as when he was writing *Hadji Murad*, 'partly with pleasure, partly against the grain and with shame'.[21] That magnificent story glorified the violent resistance and death of the Chechen chieftain and was a notable break-out from the dominantly pacifist attitude of Tolstoy in his last thirty years. It is interesting that Wittgenstein should have admired *Hadji Murad* so much, and have chosen to give a copy of it to his American friend Norman Malcolm[22] as something from which one could learn important things about human beings in war. It was, in any case, only in some respects that Wittgenstein was a Tolstoyan. He was far from being a pacifist, for instance, and he was not a vegetarian. One of his favourite

---

[20] See for instance Fanya Pascal's perceptive *Wittgenstein: A Personal Memoir* in *Ludwig Wittgenstein: Personal Recollections*, ed. Rush Rhees, Oxford 1981, p.34.
[21] Tolstoy, Diary entry for 5 August 1902.
[22] See Norman Malcolm, *Ludwig Wittgenstein: A Memoir*, Oxford 1984², pp. 94, 96.

dishes at Messrs Lyons in Petty Cury was steak-and-
kidney pie. He was still further from thoroughgoing
Buddhism, and had no mercy for exasperating flies. I do,
on the other hand, remember his feeding one of the
horses pastured on Trinity Paddocks. He brought a fat
bagful of bread and fed the horse with his right hand,
talking to him (or her, I don't recall which) in the gentlest
and tenderest tones.)

Part II of the recital consisted of five songs from the
seventeenth century onwards. The first was a dialogue
between a maidservant and a priest. It was a teasing
song. The girl asked him why his clothes were in such a
mess. He had been to the fair and the market, he said.
What had he brought for her? Some dancing shoes. When
would he give them to her? When she knew how to work.
Oh! she can sew and spin. Well then, he'll have to give
her them. But she would like to confess first. What was
her greatest sin? Loving you too much, M. le Curé. Then
we shall have to separate. No, for then I should die, M. le
Curé. Well, I shall bury you, *Simonne, ma Simonne, ma
mignonne*. Are you weeping, M. le Curé? No, for I must
sing, Simonne, my Simonne, *Requiescat in pace*, my
mignonne. Wittgenstein seemed quite amused by that
one.

Yet it was two of the remaining four that really thrilled
him. One was called 'Les Deux Notaires'. It was a duet
between two old lawyers. Maître Lebègue calls on Maître
Robin with a contract concerning a 'charming client' who
will soon be eighteen. This prompts Maître Robin to
recall the days when *they* were eighteen. They had a good
time, but, alas, they were not *notaires* then! They were
handsome, and had parties each evening. They were law
students in Paris, and bachelors, but not alas *notaires*.
And they recalled their girl friends, and how they were
adored by them. Then they were colleagues, but still not

notaires. Towards the end Lebègue suggests that they should try to look at each other without laughing. Think what people could say about them if they knew them better. His wife was tiresomely jealous. One had to put up with it. And finally M. Robin directs his attention to the contract to be signed, calling Lebègue 'très cher collègue', but adding 'farceur et grand scélérat!' ('joker ... and great big rogue!'), and warns him not to forget his contract. But *they*, in the old times, didn't bother about contracts, when they were not, alas, *notaires*! The skilfully contrasted impersonation of the two old lawyers and their high spirits in their reminiscences caught Wittgenstein's fancy, and he was clearly delighted, turning to me with a broad smile. The other song that attracted him particularly was an eighteenth-century monologue called 'Mais oui, Mesdames', which Yvette Guilbert had herself set to music. The woman was a lively person who had been jilted by her lover after he had courted her for six-and-a-half months, 'Mais oui, mais, oui'. The story she tells intermingles confessions of her passion for the man with assertions of proud independence and of mockery for the faithless rascal. The 'Mais oui, mais oui' and 'Mais oui, Mesdames' are strewn through the song and function sometimes as appeals for the sympathy of the ladies to whom she is telling her story and sometimes simply to underline facts and intentions. The sounds in their varying intonations still ring in my ears over fifty years later. Yvette Guilbert's was a brilliant *virtuoso* performance. Understandably, Wittgenstein was strongly impressed and buoyant with delight.

At the end of the whole performance he applauded with great enthusiasm. He was also anxious to visit Yvette Guilbert and to present her with a magnificent bouquet of scarlet carnations. I had already been surprised when

he had praised the piano accompaniment by a good-
looking and elegantly-dressed young woman. I imagined
that he would consider her altogether too conventionally
elegant in her dress and general appearance to be worthy
of praise on any account. That of course, was, pretty naïve
of me. On the other hand he himself was particularly
smartly dressed on that occasion, and this had already
been unexpected. And now the carnations. The whole
occasion brought out for me another side of Wittgenstein's
personality, and I found it both astonishing and
refreshing.

20

I have only recently managed to fix the exact date of the
Yvette Guilbert recital: 27 May 1938. Also recently,
however, I have discovered among old papers of mine a
letter to me from Wittgenstein dated 12 April 1938, and
the two dates make me wonder whether perhaps his
invitation to me to go to the recital may conceivably have
been as a reward for something I had done for which he
thanked me in the letter.

The letter reads as follows:

81 East Road[23]
Cambridge
12.4.38.[24]

Dear Redpath,

Our letter did wonders. – I had a letter from Keynes on Saturday morning saying that he had written a letter to Mr Gwatkin the solicitor. I saw Mr G. yesterday, and he seems very kind and helpful. I did *not*, as I said I would, ring up another solicitor on Friday but took the chance and waited for Keynes to keep his promise, and I'm glad he did.

Thank you very much indeed for your help which has proved most valuable.

So long!
Yours,
Ludwig Wittgenstein

Wittgenstein had been in touch with Maynard Keynes to enlist his advice and help about the possibility of naturalization, in view of the growing threat by the Nazis to people with Jewish blood. Wittgenstein had actually three full-blooded Jewish grandparents, though none of the three practised the Jewish religion in their maturity.[25] His paternal grandfather, Hermann Christian, a German from Saxony, had been converted to Lutheran Protestantism, and his Jewish wife, Fanny Figdor, a Viennese girl, was baptized in the same faith just before the marriage. As for Wittgenstein's maternal grandparents, the grandfather Jakob Kalmus, born in

---

[23] Wittgenstein was at that time living with Francis Skinner over Mr and Mrs Barbrook's greengrocer's shop.

[24] 12 April 1938 was a Tuesday. So Keynes's letter had apparently arrived on 9 April.

[25] For Wittgenstein's ancestry, see Brian McGuinness, op. cit., pp. 1-23.

Prague, had strong connexions with Roman Catholic converts, while the maternal grandmother, Maria Stallner, from Styria, was non-Jewish and Catholic. Wittgenstein himself was baptized as a Catholic. He was, however, acutely conscious of his Jewish blood and had an ambivalent and complicated attitude towards it, and towards the Christian overlay that had come about in the family over the last two generations. The advent of Nazism was naturally deeply disturbing to him, both because of his family in Vienna and in view of its probable effect on his own future. His vital concern was to be able to live where he could work at philosophy. I remember him asking me some time earlier in 1938 whether I thought it would be 'decent' of him to apply for naturalization. I said I thought it would be quite understandable and perfectly 'decent' for him to do so. So he told me that he was thinking of writing to Maynard Keynes to ask for his help about that. He also mentioned that he understood that Moore would soon be retiring from the Chair of Philosophy at Cambridge and that he might apply to succeed Moore. If he did, he would like Keynes to give him some support, but he would need to be ready to send Keynes some work for him to look at. Then a bit later Wittgenstein told me he had written to Keynes[26] about the naturalization possibility (and I believe also about Moore's Chair or at all events about *some* Cambridge appointment). About the naturalization, at least, Keynes evidently promised to help. The Germans invaded Austria on 13 March 1938, and so Wittgenstein was placed in an especially perilous situation, because he would now be German. Moreover he would be forced to hold a German Jewish passport, if

[26] He evidently wrote to Keynes on 18 March 1938 (see Michael Nedo & Michele Ranchetti, *Ludwig Wittgenstein*, Frankfurt-am-Main 1983, pp. 298-9).

indeed he could obtain a passport at all.[27] I believe what happened then was that Keynes had recommended a solicitor called Gwatkin, but that Wittgenstein really wanted Keynes to write specifically to Gwatkin asking him to take up his case and to act for him pretty urgently. Wittgenstein had not yet heard anything further. It was then, I think, that he asked me to come and see him and help him to decide what was the best thing to do next. He was very agitated. As far as I can remember, I suggested that he should write to Keynes a tactful letter specifically asking him to get Gwatkin to act as effectively and urgently as he could, and I remember then helping him to concoct the letter which he said 'worked wonders'. I suggested that if he did not hear from Keynes within a reasonable time he might like to consult another solicitor in London whom I could recommend. He said he would ring up this alternative solicitor and take his advice if he did not hear from Keynes within a few days. Fortunately Keynes wrote saying he had written to Gwatkin, whom Wittgenstein then saw, and so everything went ahead on that front, though he did not actually acquire British nationality till 14 April 1939 and did not receive his passport till 2 June 1939.

[27] I see now from Nedo & Ranchetti (*supra*) that Piero Sraffa wrote to Wittgenstein from King's College on 14 March 1938, warning him that if it was of 'vital importance' for him to be able to leave Austria and return to England he must not go to Vienna. He would not be let out of Austria. The frontier was now closed to the exit of Austrians and it would make no difference that he was a Lecturer at Cambridge.

21

There was another surprise in store for me in a musical context, though in this case it was only touched off by a musical topic, and its importance was more generally philosophical.

Wittgenstein called on me one afternoon at The Hermitage. I had been buying some gramophone records, after hearing them played in one of the cubicles in Miller's music shop. I cannot now remember what they were, no doubt because I was so forcibly struck by the philosophical point which Wittgenstein made. He asked me whether the records were 'any good'. Now, it was quite common at that time to answer such questions by saying 'it depends what you mean by ...'. So I replied to Wittgenstein's question with the words 'It depends what you mean by "good".' His response was rapid and decisive: '*I* mean what *you* mean.' This shook me up, and seemed to me tremendously illuminating. It still does.

22

Suddenly, during one of our conversations early in 1938, Wittgenstein asked me whether I had ever had any *tragedies* in my life. Again, true to form, I asked him what he meant by a 'tragedy'. 'Well,' he replied, 'I don't mean the death of your old grandmother at the age of 85. I mean *suicides, madness* or *quarrels*.' I said that I had been fortunate enough not to have experienced any of those terrible things.

I had no idea at the time that three of his brothers had committed suicide, and that he himself had often felt suicidal and had more than once seriously contemplated killing himself. Nor did I know that he had sometimes feared madness. As for quarrels, he seemed at times such an aggressive man that one could readily imagine that he could have been engaged in serious quarrels, but the only cases I was aware of at that time were his sharp repudiation in 1933, in a letter to the Editor of *Mind*,[28] of the account of his views given by Richard Braithwaite in an article on Cambridge philosophers in *Cambridge University Studies*,[29] and some altercation he had with Alice Ambrose in 1935, which she recounts years later in her article 'Ludwig Wittgenstein: A Portrait'.[30]

Wittgenstein's choice of *suicides, madness* and *quarrels* as examples of *tragedies* naturally struck me forcibly, despite my knowing nothing of the potency of personal reference that *suicides* and *madness* had for him in his earlier life.

Many years later, when I came to lecture in the Faculty of English at Cambridge both on Tragedy and on Theories of Tragedy, the three examples quoted by Wittgenstein often recurred to me, though they by no means exhaust the categories of Tragedy, and certainly not the ramifications of the topic, as I imagine he would have readily admitted. His remark was, however, seminal for me, and I believe it could well be seminal for others.

[28] *Mind* (1933). Wittgenstein's letter was dated 12 April 1933.
[29] ed. Harold Wright, London 1933, pp. 1-32.
[30] *Ludwig Wittgenstein: Philosophy and Language*, ed. Alice Ambrose & Morris Lazerowitz, London 1972, pp. 22-4.

23

In the Long Vacation of 1938 I was lent a set of rooms by a Johnian friend who was away for the Long Vacation. They were on the first floor of Third Court, overlooking the river. Wittgenstein came to see me a few times while I was there, and I remember a few miscellaneous things that occurred.

I had a copy of Locke's *Essay* there, and Wittgenstein and I were looking at it together. At one point we happened to look at the engraved portrait of Locke opposite the title page, and he said he thought Locke's face 'a nice face'. I agreed, but I had the feeling that he was putting a moral point and possibly trying to influence me in a moral way. I myself also admired energetic faces which might not need to be quite so moral to be worthy of admiration, and I said that I admired the face of Descartes. Wittgenstein's rejoinder was itself energetic: 'Descartes' face is that of a murderer.'

Another thing I recall was that I had a ream of blank foolscap in a packet on a high shelf. Wittgenstein noticed it, and I said I hoped to get a good deal of writing done before the end of the Long Vacation. His comment was cautionary, to say the least: 'It is damned hard to write things that make blank sheets better!'

One day I invited him to a frugal lunch there. The menu was cold tongue, potato salad and fresh tomatoes with salad cream, followed by sponge cakes steeped in orange juice, with cream and sugar. I myself was pretty hungry and showed it. But I had the idea that Wittgenstein might think me too ravenous, so I deprecated my healthy appetite. To my surprise he

thought it quite 'natural' to be so 'hungry' and we both
ate the meal heartily. We drank water. I never saw him
drink anything alcoholic.

During the summer of 1938 he showed much concern
for Czechoslovakia and was angry with the British
Government for not having talks at the highest level with
Russia but only sending relatively minor delegations to
discuss the worsening situation. I myself saw his point of
view, but I was even more concerned with the situation of
Britain, which was militarily far less well prepared in
1938 than Czechoslovakia. I had had a vivid glimpse of
this comparison in 1936, when I had visited Czechoslovakia with my mother for a summer holiday. Our time
there included a few days at Košice, in Slovakia, where
we stayed at a hotel whose Director had been an officer in
the Czechoslovak army and who took us to see various
sights in Slovakia, including the cold geyser at Herlany.
We spent much time talking to him and to a Slovak
friend of his who knew English well. We got on such good
terms that we asked the Director to come and stay
with us in London, and he spent a week or so with us in
September. One afternoon my father and I drove him out
to Windsor and we roamed round the Great Park. Near
one of the gates there was a café and we stopped there for
tea. While we were having it a company of Guards
marched past. A fine-looking body of men, I thought, but
I wondered what our friend would think of them. I had
seen a number of Czechoslovak Army units in Prague,
and it was clear that the Czechs took their armed forces
and their great fortress in Central Europe very seriously.
The Director's comment on our company of Guards was,
however, more trenchant than I had expected: 'I am
horrified,' he said. 'Their equipment is hopelessly
antiquated.' Now, I had heard reports that our
government was really concerned about the neglect of

our armed forces and was determined to make up for lost time. So, when talking with Wittgenstein two years later, I said I thought the problem was hard for Britain in view of her military weakness, and that she might have to temporize in order to gain time to re-arm. On the other hand it was a terrible thing to sacrifice the Czechs and their fortress, and it is hard to estimate the rights and wrongs of Munich, about which Wittgenstein himself told me later that the issue was 'a personal one'.

The only other clear memory I have of contacts I had with Wittgenstein in those rooms at St John's that summer was that he volunteered to post a letter for me and I declined the offer, upon which he said I was right not to trust anyone to post one's letters, though he may not have meant that seriously.

Postcript: I have just recalled another, rather more significant, moment in those rooms. The friend who lent me them had small reproduction drawings of Bernard Shaw and T.S. Eliot hanging in frames on one of the walls. I cannot remember any comment Wittgenstein made about Shaw, but about Eliot's face he remarked in a negative tone that it was 'a modern face'.

24

Also in the summer of 1938 Wittgenstein asked me if I would be willing to assist him in translating the Preface to a book which he was thinking of publishing.[31] I said I should be very glad to try to help. I had not realized what

[31] This was the book ultimately published posthumously in 1953, as *Philosophische Untersuchungen*, with an English translation by G.E.M. Anscombe under the title *Philosophical Investigations*. The Preface is dated January 1945.

an exhausting task it would be. We sat for several hours one day thinking out not only every sentence, but pretty well every word, and Wittgenstein sometimes got very worked up when he (or we) could not find words or phrases which entirely satisfied him. Time and again I found myself wishing to heaven that he would let me work on the German quite alone and present him with a version which he could then comment on and revise, but he pushed inexorably on, and though his interpositions were sometimes quite awry, as well as exasperating, one did learn something from the procedure, and it gave one an insight into Wittgenstein's fanatical care both for accuracy and for style.[32] In August 1938 he sent me a typescript.

It is interesting to compare this interim state of the Preface (which I shall call 'the interim Preface') with the final state dated seven years later. In the interim version Wittgenstein refers to 'this and the following volumes'. He had clearly in mind the vast corpus of writing he had accumulated over the past nine years, that is, since he returned to Cambridge in 1929. In the interim Preface there is, however, as yet no such phrase as 'philosophical investigations', which was to be used in the first sentence of the final state of the Preface and was, of course, to be the English title of the celebrated book finally published, posthumously, in 1953.

On the other hand the interim Preface (1938) reveals more precisely than the final state the points in time at which Wittgenstein had attempted to collect his

---

[32] When I look back on my vexation over the irksomeness of those comparatively few hours of collaboration, my feelings on that occasion seem to me *ridiculous*. I ought to have deemed it an honour to be given the chance of helping Wittgenstein on that short piece of work, which was intended to be a draft of the Preface to what was likely to be a book of considerable importance.

thoughts, written down over the years as 'remarks' (*Bemerkungen*), into a whole within which the thoughts would 'pass from one subject to another in an ordered sequence'. The interim Preface reveals that his first attempt to collect the remarks in that way had been made 'about four years ago', which suggests some time in 1934, the year when he finished dictating *The Blue Book* and started dictating *The Brown Book*, which was completed in 1935. I believe that it is very probable that the 'first attempt' was *The Blue Book*.

With regard to that 'first attempt' the interim Preface says that 'the result was unsatisfactory' but goes on to say that he then 'made various further attempts'. What were these? It seems most probable that one of them was embodied in *The Brown Book*, since the interim Preface declares that two years later (i.e. presumably in 1936) he had 'arrived at the conclusion that it was all in vain' and that he 'ought to give up any such attempt'. The question remains, however, what further attempt, if any, besides *The Brown Book*, he made between his 'first attempt' (most probably in 1934) and his conclusion (presumably in 1936) that it was useless to try any more to collect his thoughts into an ordered sequence. The 1945 Preface leaves the question unsolved. It doesn't say when the first attempt was made but simply states: 'After several unsuccessful attempts to weld my results[33] together into such a whole, I realised that I should never succeed.' The word 'several' certainly implies *more than two*, and thus the statement in the 1945 Preface at least goes so far as to imply that he made at least three attempts before he gave up and resigned himself to achieving only 'philosophical remarks'. The interim Preface, indeed,

---

[33] An interesting stylistic improvement – the characteristic engineering metaphor.

seems to go further by referring to 'various further attempts' after the first and before the abandonment of any further attempt. Now, one could incline to the view that when he wrote the interim Preface he probably had a clearer idea than several years later of just how many attempts he had made between 1934 and late 1936, but in any case both Prefaces agree that there were *at least* three attempts. If one was *The Blue Book* and another *The Brown Book*, which was the third, even if there was not actually also a fourth? The answer appears to be that a third attempt was a revision of *The Brown Book*. Professor von Wright has indicated that in August 1936 Wittgenstein began such a revision in German and that he called the revision *Philosophische Untersuchungen* (i.e. *Philosophical Investigations*).[34] He adds, however, that Wittgenstein abandoned work on that revision and made a fresh start in the autumn of 1936. Thus it turns out that, as the interim 1938 Preface implied, Wittgenstein made four attempts to collect his remarks into an ordered sequence.

Another question arises from the interim 1938 Preface. In the third paragraph Wittgenstein announces that he is beginning 'these publications' with 'the fragment' of his last attempt to arrange his philosophical thoughts in an ordered sequence. What was (or is) this 'fragment', and how exactly is it related to Part I of *Philosophical Investigations*? Part I was finished in 1945. Professor von Wright has provided the further useful information that what Wittgenstein wrote when he made a fresh start in the autumn of 1936 was substantially identical with the first 188 sections of *Philosophical Investigations* in its printed form. That could well be the 'fragment' he was

---

[34] G.H. von Wright, A Biographical Sketch, as printed in N. Malcolm, *Ludwig Wittgenstein: A Memoir*, Oxford 1984, pp. 13-14.

referring to in the interim (August 1938) Preface. If it *was* the 'fragment' it was somewhat less than half of Part I of the *Philosophical Investigations* (roughly 75 pages out of 172). It could be plausibly argued, then, that he wrote those 75 pages between the autumn of 1936 and August 1938, the date of the interim Preface, i.e. in nearly two years (40 pages a year, say). That might seem slow, considering that this final attempt had *The Brown Book* and also his German revision of it as some sort of basis to work from. Yet revision which involves re-arrangement can be very sticky. Moreover we need to take into account what other things he was doing during that period.

As I said earlier, Wittgenstein was in Cambridge in 1936 till the summer, when he went on a short holiday to France and then to his hut in Norway, where he remained till the end of the year. It seems, then, that it was that autumn, while he was in Norway, that he cut loose from simply writing a revision of *The Brown Book* and started on Part I of *Philosophical Investigations*. Then he came back to Cambridge for a week or so in January 1937 and went straight back to Norway, from which he did not return to Cambridge until the end of 1937. Early in May, however, he was in Vienna and later in England, returning to Norway in mid-August and remaining there till mid-December, and then returning to Vienna for Christmas with his family. He seems therefore to have had a month or two in Norway late in 1936 and a little over six months there in 1937 to work on less than half Part I of *Philosophical Investigations* (i.e. about 75 pages of print). In January 1938 he started to lecture twice a week for two hours each day, on the foundations of mathematics. Even if he did nothing further on the 'fragment' before August 1938, however – if that 'fragment' was, indeed, Sections 1 – 188 of Part I of

Philosophical Investigations – it had taken him eight months or more to write those 75 pages (9 pages a month). This slow rate may be connected with something he told me early in 1938: that he had spent 'most of the time' in Norway in 1936 and 1937 'feeling depressed'. This may well have been an exaggeration, but it may have corresponded, in fair measure at least, to reality. Yet we may well need to bear in mind that it is more than possible that Wittgenstein was deliberately writing very slowly and concentratedly. We might do well to regard as relevant in this context Wittgenstein's aphorism (penned in 1938): 'In philosophy the winner of the race is the one who can run most slowly. Or: the one who gets there last.'[35]

25

In 1938 my father had come to be more and more firmly convinced that Europe was heading for war. He therefore decided to sell our house in London, and since I was the only child in the family and was now based in Cambridge my parents decided to move to Cambridge. We eventually settled on a house in Madingley Road called 'Longfield' and moved in during the autumn.

In the early summer I had been elected Honorary Secretary of the Moral Science Club from October. Broad was re-elected President and Moore Chairman. I arranged a programme for the Michaelmas Term, which seemed to me pretty reasonable: the speakers were

[35] 'Im Rennen der Philosophie gewinnt, wer am langsamsten laufen kann. Oder: der, der das Ziel zuletzt erreicht.' L. Wittgenstein, *Vermischte Bemerkungen*, Herausgegeben von Georg Henrik von Wright, unter Mitarbeit von Heikki Nyman, with translation by Peter Winch, Frankfurt-am-Main 1977; Oxford 1980, p. 14/14c.

Harold Jeffreys, Gilbert Ryle, Richard Braithwaite, Sir Arthur Eddington, John Wisdom, Alfred Ewing and a Polish lady, Maria Lutman-Kokoszynska, from Wroclaw, whom I had met at the International Congress in Paris the year before and who had been received by Newnham as a visiting scholar. I gather that Wittgenstein wrote to Moore saying he didn't think much of the programme, but he didn't tell me that at the time, and he could easily have done so, as he was already back at 81 East Road, though he was evidently far from well, and under great strain because of the situation of his family now that the Nazis were in power in Austria. He was generally rather prickly at that time, and during the next few months. In my view he was sometimes right and sometimes wrong in what he did. When he came to the Eddington meeting (10 November 1938), which was held in our house in Madingley Road, he was obviously discontented at having to come some distance to the meeting, and when he came in at the front door he never greeted me but walked straight past in a boorish kind of way and on into our library and sat down. It may not have occurred to him that I arranged the venue at our house in Madingley Road to suit the convenience of Eddington who lived in the Observatory nearby. He did subsequently take a considerable part in the discussion and attacked Eddington's views very vigorously, as did Alister Watson. Moore was in the chair. Braithwaite was also present and said how good a meeting he thought it had been. But I had incurred Wittgenstein's further displeasure. This time he was quite justified. I had been writing long and careful minutes of Moral Science Club meetings, because I thought the details of the discussions might well be valuable for posterity. After the Eddington meeting, at which I had read out the rather lengthy minutes of the previous meeting, I received a scathing rebuke from

Wittgenstein. He said that the reading of lengthy minutes before a meeting dulls the minds of those present and impedes the opening of the new discussion. I saw his point at once and decided to have short minutes for reading out but a longer record of the papers, which could be kept in the minute book for reference, and I continued to try to do that for as much of the academical year as I could afford the time and energy.

Later in the academical year 1938-39, however, he caused me further difficulty. He was much in favour of having a good many 'starred meetings' in Moral Science Club programmes. 'Starred meetings' were those which excluded anyone whose name appeared in the University Lecture List. Such meetings bore an asterisk in the printed programmes. Now, it may surprise some readers that he was much in favour of a good many 'starred meetings', since there were evidently rumours in 1940 that the starring of meetings was largely directed *against* him, because he tended to monopolise discussions at non-starred meetings.[36] Whatever may have been the case in 1940, in 1939 he brought considerable pressure upon me as Secretary to *increase* the number of starred meetings. The first three meetings in the Lent Term 1939 were therefore, at his instigation, arranged as starred. They formed a series of discussions on 'Sense-data and Physical Objects'. Moore opened the first discussion on 19 January, Casimir Lewy the second on 26 January and Yorick Smythies the third on 2 February. Moore himself took the chair on 19 January and again on 26 January and Douglas Gasking on 2 February. As Secretary I was present at all those meetings and indeed at all the meetings in that academical year. The next two

[36] See Wolfe Mays, 'Recollections of Wittgenstein', in *Ludwig Wittgenstein: The Man and his Philosophy*, ed. K.T. Fann, New Jersey & Hassocks 1967, p. 82.

meetings were non-starred: Alister Watson on 'Incomplete Symbols' and Derek Prince on 'The Use of a Word'. Wittgenstein intervened considerably in the discussion of Prince's paper, attacking part of it vigorously. Looking back on the programme for that Term, I find it remarkable that at the next meeting (on 23 February 1939), which was advertised as 'starred' and at which Wittgenstein himself opened a discussion on 'Why do Philosophers often ask the meaning of some quite common words?', Smythies, in whose rooms the discussion was held, was allowed to bring two 'guests' (no doubt with Wittgenstein's permission and, I imagine, also his encouragement), both of whose names appeared in the University Lecture List: Braithwaite and Ewing. 'Why not Broad?' one might reasonably ask. I cannot help thinking in retrospect that I was being used by Wittgenstein for some kind of manoeuvres the purpose of which I was not fully aware of. I was myself in the chair at the meeting, but I cannot remember why I was asked to chair it. On the other hand Wittgenstein was quite right in believing that discussions opened by students and attended only by students were often very good and less inhibited, and I also supported his view that papers should be short and their scope restricted to a few points if they were to be dealt with adequately in the one-and-a-half to two hours available for the meeting. It was quite clear to me, though, that Wittgenstein did not like Broad (though he admitted that he was a just man), and I encountered another of his dislikes when arranging the programme for the Easter Term 1939. Some members of the Faculty had suggested that Professor Susan Stebbing, the logician, should be asked to give a paper. Wittgenstein was not at all keen, but he hit on the idea of strongly urging me, if she accepted, to make the meeting a starred one. This seemed to me a rather awkward thing to do with regard to the holder of a prestigious London Chair, but I agreed to do this provided I wrote first to Professor Stebbing asking her whether she would mind if the meeting were a starred meeting. I wrote her accordingly, and she wrote back to say she didn't mind. However, Braithwaite when he saw the programme telephoned me to say he was surprised that Professor Stebbing's meeting was starred. I explained that she said she didn't mind. But then Braithwaite wrote her saying how sorry he was that the meeting was starred and that he therefore would not be able to hear her paper. She then evidently replied to Braithwaite saying she was sorry too, as she would have liked him to be there. Upon this Braithwaite wrote to me an angry letter accusing me of being dictatorial, and also of lying when I said she had told me that she didn't mind. This was all very tiresome, and it soured my relations with Braithwaite, while I resented Wittgenstein's insistence that Professor Stebbing's meeting should be starred. I regretted that I had not been more resistant to Wittgenstein's steamrollering, and I became more independent in my behaviour. This sometimes annoyed Wittgenstein, who described me as 'playing the devil'. I find it hard to recall now specific instances which made him say that, but I must have annoyed him from time to time. I do remember one occasion when he said he would not like not to be liked, and I rather maliciously asked him what would he feel if someone had *contempt* for him. His answer to that was that he wouldn't care. I thought he probably imagined that there was no danger that such a case would arise.

I believe it may have been one of the times when he thought I was 'playing the devil' that made him take a verbal revenge in one of his *Lectures and Conversations on Aesthetics, Psychology and Religious Belief* by saying

Ludwig Wittgenstein

'Suppose we boil Redpath' (which some people have said will have earned me immortality – I hope it will not be the eternity of the damned!). Yet, if that was a case of verbal revenge, I must have been 'playing the devil' already in 1938, for it was then that Wittgenstein gave those lectures – well before the Stebbing meeting.

Ironically enough, the starred meeting on 23 February 1939 at which Wittgenstein spoke on 'Philosophy', and for which I was in the chair, seemed to me to show him at his philosophical best. He may well have been in especially good form, since it was shortly after he had been elected to succeed Moore as Professor of Philosophy. The election had been made on 10 February and this had been announced on the 11th. At all events I was myself thrilled with Wittgenstein's talk on 23 February. It was in Yorick Smythies's rooms in King's, and Wittgenstein had a small blackboard placed on an easel and used it to write up one or two points he wished to make. The talk had arisen partly out of a paper which Derek Prince had given to the Club the week before. Wittgenstein began by asking members of the audience: 'Why do philosophers ask the meaning of quite ordinary words?' (he was evidently thinking of such words as 'time', 'number', 'one') 'Have they forgotten it?' Various answers were given. One was that they were asking for a definition, or at least trying to find out whether there can be a definition of the word concerned. Wittgenstein took up this answer and asked how a definition acts as a coherent account of the use of a word. He thought one might say that a definition draws together the usages of words and gave as an example how Augustine when he asks for the meaning of a word collects instances of it. He reminds himself of those instances. But, Wittgenstein went on, if a definition is an account of the meaning, isn't it queer that people should forget it? For, after all, surely a

82

definition is a very simple thing? Must there not be a technique of working with symbols so that the definition seems to show the exact position of the word concerned with respect to all these symbols? Suppose one defines 'number' (or 'one') as Frege did,[37] has one given a full account? No, he insisted, since there are actual uses of numbers which are not accounted for by it, e.g. counting people. Definition is just one peculiar account of the use of a word. Only if one has mastered the technique of the language concerned will one learn the word from the definition. In that sense, he stated, a coherent account of a word is *not* given by a definition. It would be easy enough to define 'cap' by sense-data, but it wouldn't lead anywhere.

But why does a philosopher *want* a coherent account of the meaning at all? Can one say that he wants to describe the relation between one type of word and another type? Partly, in Wittgenstein's view. Augustine found it extremely hard to discover what time was: the essence of time. Why was he puzzled? Wittgenstein cited a passage from Heinrich Hertz's *The Principles of Mechanics*, in which Hertz wrote that people ask about the essence of matter,[38] etc., because a lot of defining criteria have been

---

[37] Since Frege laid down as a fundamental principle that we must never try to define the meaning of a word in isolation, but only as it is used in a proposition, it is not surprising that it is hard to pin down in Frege a definition of 'Number' *tout court*. The nearest one comes upon one is perhaps on p. 117 of Frege's *Die Grundlagen der Arithmetik*, Breslau 1884, which J.L. Austin translates as follows: 'The Number which belongs to the concept F is the extension of the concept "Concept equal to the concept F", where a concept F is called equal to a concept G if there exists the possibility of one-to-one correlation' (Frege, *The Foundations of Arithmetic*, tr. J.L. Austin, Oxford 1950). If this is to be taken as the definition of 'number' it would, indeed, at least not readily lend itself to counting people!

[38] Actually the passage from Hertz is not about *matter*, but about *force* and *electricity*; but that doesn't affect the issue. The point

heaped upon those notions, and these criteria are in
conflict. This irritates our mind and makes us ask 'What
is the essence of so-and-so?' The answer is not provided
by giving further criteria, according to Hertz, but by
giving fewer criteria. When the contradictions are
avoided the question is not answered but the mind, no
longer perplexed, ceases to ask the questions. Wittgenstein said that that passage from Hertz seemed to
him to sum up philosophy.

He went on to say that nothing is more characteristic of
philosophy than to ask oneself the same question a

Wittgenstein was making is the same as Hertz's. It is perhaps worth
quoting the whole passage from Hertz in the English translation of
Hertz's *The Principles of Mechanics*, tr. by D.E. Jones and J.T. Walley,
London and New York 1899. The passage occurs on pp. 7 and 8:
'Weighty evidence [of confusion] seems to be furnished by the
statements which one hears with wearisome frequency, that the
nature of force is still a mystery, that one of the chief problems of
physics is the investigation of the nature of force, and so on. In the
same way electricians are continually attacked as to the nature of
electricity. Now, why is it that people never in this way ask what is
the nature of gold, or what is the nature of velocity? Is the nature of
gold better known to us than that of electricity, or the nature of
velocity better than that of force? Can we by our conceptions, by our
words, completely represent the nature of any thing? Certainly not. I
fancy the difference must lie in this. With the terms 'velocity' and
'gold' we connect a large number of relations to other terms; and
between all these relations we find no contradictions which offend us.
We are therefore satisfied and ask no further questions. But we have
accumulated around the terms 'force' and 'electricity' more relations
than can be completely reconciled amongst themselves. We have an
obscure feeling of this and want to have things cleared up. Our
confused wish finds expression in the confused question as to the
nature of force and electricity. But the answer which we want is not
really an answer to this question. It is not by finding out more and
fresh relations and connections that it can be answered; but by
removing the contradictions existing between those already known,
and thus perhaps by reducing their number. When these painful
contradictions are removed, the question as to the nature of force will
not have been answered; but our minds, no longer vexed, will cease to
ask illegitimate questions.'

thousand times. But sometimes a person stops. What makes one stop? Sometimes one is given a new analogy, which replaces an old analogy. Wittgenstein said he had often pointed out that a child is puzzled when a word is seen to have two different meanings. If this is to cease to be puzzling it must be surrounded by other cases.

At this point he went back to a discussion the week before of Derek Prince's paper which *inter alia* rejected the view that 'the meaning of a word' was equivalent to 'the use to which the word is put'. He contended that in a vast number of cases it is possible to replace 'the meaning of a word' by 'the use of a word', and he asked in what way it was useful to do this. Casimir Lewy rightly replied that it might get rid of the idea that the meaning of a word is a picture attached to the word. Wittgenstein then amplified the point by asking how the picture and the use hang together, and suggesting that the connexion between picture and use was entirely paralleled by the connexion between ostensive definition and use. If we ask 'What is a zebra?', does someone's pointing to a picture of a zebra involve that he uses the word 'zebra' as we do? The connexion of an image or picture and use is that as a matter of fact in an enormous number of cases to one particular picture or image there corresponds one particular use, and where it does *not*, which is also in an immense number of cases, puzzlement arises. So, to the question why it is in a great number of cases profitable to ask for the use of a word and not the meaning Wittgenstein's answer was: because *meaning* suggests one object, whereas *use* suggests a number of objects spread out in time.

Finally he intimated that the dictum 'In a great number of cases it is advisable to put "use of a word" for "meaning of a word" ' is a slogan. Sometimes the slogan is ridiculed, sometimes it is boosted: in both cases, in his opinion, wrongly. If one does philosophy it is natural that one should come to certain sorts of step which it is advisable to take. Philosophical investigations are tedious and difficult and slip the memory. Slogans are easy and stick in the memory. If the *use* of the slogan goes, but the slogan remains, it is *ridiculous*.

I believe the audience was much impressed with this talk and I certainly was myself. It seemed to me to put in general terms, and with reference to specific instances, a central point in Wittgenstein's philosophy, and all in not more than half an hour.

26

It was towards the end of the Lent Term 1939 that two new people appeared at one of Wittgenstein's lectures. Knowing his aversion to such surprise invasions, I wondered what would happen. If I remember rightly, Wittgenstein asked them what they were doing there and whether they intended to follow the course. They didn't really answer his question, at all events to his satisfaction. Indeed he hardly gave them time to, for he added, quite uncompromisingly: 'I don't want any tourists here, you know!' They were, however, allowed to stay for the rest of the lecture.

One of the newcomers was Georg Henrik von Wright from Helsinki who nearly twenty years later was to succeed Wittgenstein as Professor of Philosophy at Cambridge. He wrote to Wittgenstein shortly after the dramatic incident at the lecture, explaining that Broad, then Chairman of the Faculty Board, had given him permission to attend lectures and classes in philosophy. Wittgenstein wrote a reply[39] explaining why such invasions disturbed him. Anyone coming in the middle or at the end of term could not possibly understand what he was driving at, and he would naturally worry about that and could not properly concentrate on the difficult matters he was trying to explain. He added that he could not, as many people did, write his lectures beforehand and read them to his listeners. If he did that newcomers would not disturb him, but as he had to think things out afresh while talking he was very easily disturbed. He suggested that if von Wright wished to come to the classes he should start at the beginning of next term. In a P.S., however, he suggested that von Wright should come to see him at 81 East Road, at 4.30 the next day. It might be easier to explain than by writing. Von Wright went, and that was the prelude to a close friendship.

I came to know von Wright very soon after that, and we had several inspiring talks walking up and down our garden at home. In May 1939 he gave an excellent paper to the Moral Science Club on 'The Justification of Induction', which was warmly applauded by all present. Alas, our contact was broken during the war, but we have had some fruitful conversations periodically since then.

Wittgenstein told me early on that he set a high value on von Wright's qualities, and he warmly recommended him as his successor in the Cambridge Chair of Philosophy in 1948.

Who was the other intruder in Wittgenstein's lecture at the end of the Lent Term 1939? I understand from von Wright that he cannot remember who that second person was. My own memory is somewhat hazy as to exactly who were at Wittgenstein's lectures in the academical year 1938-39. I believe Casimir Lewy, Georg Henrik von

[39] Letter to v. Wright, 9 March 1939, reprinted in *The Cambridge Review*, 28 February 1983.

Wright, Norman Malcolm, Yorick Smythies, Francis
Kitto, Alister Watson, and Richard Bosanquet were
there. There was also A.M. Turing, the mathematical
logician from King's, who eventually created a stir by his
researches on the relations between computers and
human intelligence. (See his article in *Mind* 1950.)

27

During 1939 Wittgenstein was often in touch with me,
and he sometimes came to our house so that we could
talk. Some time in the spring or early summer we walked
up and down the garden. There was a lawn on the south
side of the house, and at the south end of the lawn there
was a wilderness of tall grasses interspersed with
flowering bushes. The lawn continued into the wilderness as a wide grass path along which two people could
walk comfortably abreast, and even three, not quite so
comfortably. I was very fond of walking along that path
(either alone or with one or two companions) to the end of
it, where it was cut off by a transverse gravel path which
swung in from the west side of the garden. Beyond that
path on the south side were some patches for vegetables
and soft fruit, bounded by iron railings and a central
gate, which gave on to tennis courts and a playing field.
The first time Wittgenstein walked down the garden with
me and we came to the wide grass path he stopped and
exclaimed: 'That is all wrong!' I asked what he meant. He
said that the grass path ought to have been *narrow*, so
that only one person could walk along it. 'Anyone with
any taste would realise that,' he remarked. I was far from
convinced by that downright assertion, and I also felt
nettled by his reflection on my taste, as well as the taste

of those who laid out the path. However, we continued along it and eventually reached the gravel path. When we did, Wittgenstein burst out: 'That is what it was crying out for!' And then he amplified his view. The path along which we had walked should either have been a *narrow* grass path *or* a wide *gravel* path. I was still unconvinced, and I was still rather annoyed. I did, however, see that the gravel might have been more convenient when the ground was wet. Yet the idea of the lawn being continued by the wide gravel path did not appeal to me aesthetically. And I did not take to Wittgenstein's bullying manner.

It was also probably some time during the spring of 1939 that Wittgenstein came to tea with us to hear Basil Willey and me play some Mozart piano duets. My parents had invited Basil, and when I told Wittgenstein that we should be playing the duets and asked him if he would care to come he said he would. Basil was not only a gifted pianist but was also by then King Edward VII Professor of English Literature at Cambridge, a fact which is relevant to the episode I am about to recount. After tea we played several Mozart duets, including the Theme and Variations in G Major (K. 501). We had barely started that piece when, in the eighth bar, Basil, who was playing the bass part, executed the closing arpeggio in a light-hearted, even jaunty way. Wittgenstein was livid: 'Is that a joke or something?' he rapped out, much to my embarrassment. Fortunately Basil, who was a wonderfully tolerant man, with moreover a refined sense of humour, let the comment pass, and we went on through the rest of the theme and all the variations without any further intervention from Wittgenstein. Whether he thought that we had played more or less decently, or he had regretted his hurtful sally, or whether there was some other explanation I never knew. As to my own reaction to the episode, it was, as often, mixed. I respected his intense concern for Mozart's music, and his views as to how it should be played. On the other hand I hated the idea of Basil's feelings being so brutally bashed. Yet, in the end, one might say, was there much harm done?

Early in 1939 I was having considerable difficulties with parts of my PhD dissertation, and I was almost in despair about some of what I had written, especially about the mind-body problems and what Wittgenstein would think of the ways I had tried to tackle them. My father suggested that it might be a good idea to go round to see Wittgenstein at 81 East Road. (He was not on the telephone there.) I went round, and Wittgenstein offered to come to our house, read any part of my dissertation which I wanted him to look at and give his opinion as to how it was getting on. He did so, and when I showed him some parts with which I had not been at all happy he read them carefully and was very kind and encouraging, saying that they were quite decent and that I seemed to be rather like a 'Scholastic' in some of what I had written. That was a great relief to me. On the other hand, quite rightly, Wittgenstein asked me whether I had been showing any signs of my worries to my father and mother, and when I admitted that I *had* he said that that was preposterous of me and that I ought to keep that sort of worry to myself and not bother them. I thought his view correct, though I was in quite a state, because I was planning to submit the dissertation in August or September and knew that Wittgenstein was expecting to go abroad within a few months and would not be available for further advice. I had the advice of two excellent Supervisors, Moore and Broad, but I had been concerned as to what his opinion would be.

As already mentioned, in February 1939 Wittgenstein

had been elected by the University to succeed Moore in the Chair of Philosophy in October,[40] and he acquired British nationality in April that year. After that he had in June gone to Vienna, and in July to Berlin, and then back through England to New York to make some arrangements concerning Wittgenstein family affairs. He returned to Cambridge in mid-August. He was still living at 81 East Road.

Some time shortly after that he told me that he would be going to the Fellowship Admission Dinner at Trinity early in October. There would be several other Fellows admitted, including Research Fellows from the recent annual election. But he would be a *'Professorial* Fellow' he said, with typical half-mock pride (the sort of mixed feeling that I had encountered on another occasion when he had in conversation referred to himself as 'a champ'). Well, he wondered whether I might be able to lend him some tails, a white waistcoat and a stiff shirt and white tie for the occasion. He thought we were about the same size and shape. If he might borrow these things, could he come round and try them on? I said, certainly. He said he would, of course, have the waistcoat, shirt and tie laundered. So we arranged a time, and he came to our house. My father was at home at the time, and found it all rather amusing. I took Wittgenstein up to a small bedroom, which was really a dressing room next to my parents' bedroom. He said he would like me to see if the

[40] It may be interesting to readers to know who the Electors were who elected Wittgenstein on 10 February 1939 to the Professorship of Philosophy from 1 October 1939 in succession to Professor G.E. Moore. They were: Dr Cornford, Professor Collingwood, Professor Hardy, Mr Keynes, Professor L.J. Russell, Dr Broad, Dr Kemp Smith and Professor Price. Earl Russell had been an Elector until 3 February 1939, but then resigned, Professor L.J. Russell was appointed in his place. (*Cambridge University Reporter*, 14 February 1939, p. 626.)

whole outfit looked reasonable, but I cannot distinctly remember what happened next. Perhaps I asked him to knock on the communicating door when he was ready, and I would go in and give him my opinion, or perhaps he asked me to stay with him while he dressed. In any case I eventually made the inspection. While I was carrying it out, however, I heard my father come into my parents' bedroom next door. He had innocently, but rather rashly, thought that Wittgenstein might value his opinion as to whether the outfit looked good enough for the great occasion. So he knocked on the dressing-room door and asked whether he could come and inspect. Not knowing Wittgenstein's ways he could hardly have anticipated the reaction, which even somewhat surprised me. Wittgenstein flew off the handle. 'No,' he shouted in a kind of panic. 'Don't come in!' My father accordingly retired. I finished the inspection, but Wittgenstein was also able to satisfy himself about the front view, as there was a mirror in the wardrobe. The garments seemed to fit remarkably well, and in due course they were all packed up, and Wittgenstein wore them at the dinner. Afterwards he had the laundering done by the Wellbrook Laundry at Girton. Wittgenstein thought highly of it, and later my family transferred to it. It was an enterprise of which Edith Chrystal, a Fellow of Newnham, a most august and charming Scottish lady, was a Director.

28

I submitted my PhD dissertation in the Faculty of Moral Sciences in September 1939. It had been completed early in August and then typed, and Wittgenstein had suggested to me as an appropriate epigraph an admirable quotation from Augustine's *Confessions*:

> Et multi ante nos vitam istam agentes praestruxerant aerumnosas vias per quas transire cogebamur multiplicato labore et dolore filiis Adam. (I.ix)

> (And many men before us in charge of this mode of life[41] had contrived toilsome paths along which we were forced to go, so multiplying work and suffering for the sons of Adam.)

The title of my dissertation was: *Four Philosophical Controversies engaged in by Leibniz and certain other Philosophers of the late 17th and early 18th Centuries*. It was an attempt to rewrite a piece of history of philosophy making use of a concentrated examination of the terms (e.g. the slippery key term 'substance') in which the apparently conflicting positions were stated by the philosophers concerned and, among other things, to try to say how far such conflicting contentions (e.g. as to the number of existent substances) could be correctly called 'merely verbal'. I had some talks with Wittgenstein around this time, and he seemed to know what I was trying to do. Moore certainly did.

My examiners were L.J. Russell of Birmingham and J.L. Austin of Oxford, and I was awarded the Degree in January 1940.

The war had started on 3 September 1939. I had been on a short holiday in France while my dissertation was being typed. I stayed for a week or so in Auvergne with my friend Roland Cailleux[42] and hurtled back when war seemed imminent. Paris was blacked out and the atmos-

---

[41] i.e. education
[42] Roland Cailleux was a medical specialist at Châtel-Guyon whom I had met at Cambridge, where we started a close friendship, which lasted till his death in 1980.

phere was tense, but I arrived home safely with a couple of days to spare.

Like so many people I had anticipated war for some time. I had been quite active in the OTC, first in the Infantry and then as a Gunner, and I had taken not only Certificate A, but also Certificate B, which was supposed to qualify one for a commission after further training. I spent one morning early in September walking round Cambridge with a friend who had decided to be a pacifist. I respected his position, but I could not share it. I decided to volunteer at once for the Army and went to the recruiting board, which recommended me for training for a commission in the Royal Artillery. At the medical examination, however, I was found to have something wrong with my back, and I was rejected for the time being. Wittgenstein commiserated with me, but I said I was determined to get myself fit by taking a good deal of exercise and to present myself for another medical examination after an appropriate lapse of time.

Meanwhile I undertook supervision in English for some of the Colleges, and I continued to attend Wittgenstein's classes. I was still doing so in the Lent Term 1940, since I remember Wittgenstein, before one of his lectures began, sitting in a deck chair and congratulating me on my 'Doctorate'.

One day I asked him why he never stated any political views or discussed politics in any of his lectures. His reply was interesting. He said he *could* not do so but that one day he would give a lecture or talk explaining *why* he could not. He never gave such a lecture or talk while I was still attending his classes.

I have an Easter card which he sent me dated 21 March 1940. It is a conventional, deliberately 'unaesthetic' picture of chickens and white and coloured flowers, and coloured eggs, with the title 'Easter Gladness' and a short printed poem:

> As Easter flowers and Easter sunshine
> Gladden all the earth today,
> So may the message that
>   It brings us –
> Keep us happy all Life's way.

In a moment of Puckish humour he had enlivened the card by writing neatly below the picture the words: L. Wittgenstein pinx.

Wittgenstein was evidently in a chirpy mood around that time. Shortly after Easter 1940 he sent me another postcard which expressed a similar spirit. He and Francis Skinner had gone down for a week-end at Hastings to have a blow of sea air together. He was always anxious about Francis's health and thought that this would set him up a bit. I don't know where they actually stayed, but he sent me back a black-and-white postcard photograph of two windmills. Above one of the windmills he had written 'Francis's house' and above the other 'my house' and drawn two arrows pointing down to the supposed respective abodes. I was quite taken in that time though it was after all not utterly unreasonable to believe that each of them was occupying a windmill. Yet not long after he returned to Cambridge, when I thanked him for the card and said what fun it must have been to have had a windmill each to stay in, he laughed at me for being so gullible. I didn't take umbrage at all but found it odd that he should consider it so implausible that he and Francis, far from hidebound in their mode of life, should have spent their week-end based in a couple of windmills.

I believe it must have been soon after this that my mother invited Wittgenstein and Francis Skinner to dinner with us at Longfield. My father was away at the time on war work in the Ministry of Aircraft Production. My mother thought Francis Skinner a very agreeable young man, and she was sorry for his disability. I cannot remember much about the occasion except for two things. One is that my mother and Wittgenstein got involved in some kind of political discussion. My mother was fairly liberal-minded about politics and seemed to be in agreement with Wittgenstein about the failure of the British Government to take the Czech and Russian anti-Hitler potential more seriously before Munich; but she was not idealistic about the industry of British workmen in general, and Wittgenstein thought she went too far in her criticisms. Yet the discussion didn't become heated, and Wittgenstein seemed to be in a good mood and also to be glad that my mother had invited Francis too. Indeed the second detail I remember is that for sweet my mother had prepared a pudding of semolina or ground rice with pears floating on top in their syrup. Two cloves were stuck in each pear for eyes. When the dish arrived on the table Wittgenstein was obviously pleased with the droll sight and nudged Francis to make him take due note of it, which he did.

Other instances have been recorded of Wittgenstein taking pleasure in particular foods and food dishes, and he seems to have particularly appreciated well-meant, homely and unostentatious care about such things.

On the other hand I distinctly recall his saying to me once that one should never thank anybody for a meal!

In May 1940 I was still taking exercise and trying to get fit, but I felt I should be making some greater contribution to the national effort, so I applied to become an Air Raid Warden until I could get into the Army. I was accepted. My health seemed to me to be excellent now, so I again volunteered for the Army and had a fresh medical examination, which I passed. I was finally accepted in

August 1940 for training as an Officer in the Royal
Artillery, and placed on the Reserve. It took ages,
however, for me to be posted to my unit, and I continued
to serve as an Air Raid Warden and also to teach for
Colleges. During that time I had a fair number of
philosophical discussions with Wittgenstein. I told him
that I hoped to be able to apply his philosophical method
to some problems other than those he had specifically
tackled. I mentioned as examples the conflict about
epigenesis and pre-formation in biology, the free-will
tangle, disputes in literary criticism and the ramifications about the concept of intelligence in relation to
lower animals. He seemed to approve of the idea. With
regard to animal intelligence he spoke highly of Köhler's
book on the mentality of apes and monkeys and called
Buffon 'a colossal chap'.

I had stopped going to Wittgenstein's classes in June
1940. That of course was the month France collapsed. I
wanted to get posted to my Army unit. Until then I
wanted to continue my supervisions in English, and I
needed to spend time in preparing my teaching, which
however it was understood I should break off if I had to
join my unit. So I could not, alas, afford the time to follow
Wittgenstein's classes regularly, and there was no point
in sporadic attendance, as we agreed. I also stopped
going to Moral Science Club meetings, as I was generally
on duty as an Air Raid Warden on those evenings. As a
result I missed many meetings when Wittgenstein was in
the Chair, and one in October 1940 when he gave a talk
on 'Other Minds'.

Wittgenstein himself, however, was concerned to
render some more obviously practical service to Britain
besides his work as a Professor and writer of philosophy,
and he therefore applied in 1941 for work as a dispensary
porter at Guy's Hospital. I do not know exactly when he

started work there: but Messrs Nedo and Ranchetti say November 1941.[43] If that is correct it was just after the death of Francis Skinner, which was on 11 October. That must have been a tremendous blow to Wittgenstein, however much he may have anticipated an early death for Francis. I didn't know about Francis's death at the time. I had at last been posted in May 1941 as an Officer Cadet in the Royal Artillery for training at the HAC OCTU at Alton Towers in North Staffordshire. Wittgenstein apparently did very fine work in the dispensary at Guy's,[44] especially on ointments, and later on wound shock at the Royal Victoria Infirmary at Newcastle, where he worked right till the end of the war.

As far as I can remember I never saw Wittgenstein again until 1949, and I did not correspond with him till 1948. He had closer friends than me, and I had closer friends than him, and we both had our blood-relations. I did, however, receive a word of greeting from him through Yorick Smythies, who paid me a visit in the winter of 1941-42 when I was stationed in Oxford.

29

When I was demobilised in the summer of 1946 I at once put my mind to working for the Bar Final Examination with the object of practising at the Bar. I had taken all of Part I before the war and was longing to get back to law and embark on my chosen career. I had been asked by the army to stay on, but I was bent on a legal, and possibly a political, career. (Incidentally, Wittgenstein had known

[43] op. cit., p. 359.
[44] For an interesting account see J.R. Henderson, *Ludwig Wittgenstein and Guy's Hospital*, Guy's Hospital Reports 1973, pp. 185-93.

of my political ambitions before the war, but had sternly
though salutarily declared that to be a good politician one
needed to have a good purge.)[45] At all events I worked
hard for the Bar Finals and took them in the spring of
1948. Shortly afterwards I was called to the Bar at The
Middle Temple. Then, with the help of my father, who
had served on a number of occasions as an expert witness
in legal cases and so come to know various eminent
members of the Bar, I looked round for chambers in
which to do the year's pupilage required before one could
be nominally qualified to practise. I was fortunate
enough to find a pupil's place in very good chambers in
Hare Court, for the year starting in Autumn 1948, but
only for the one year, as the chambers were small and my
place was already booked for the year after that. I had
about five months to spare before taking up that place,
and I considered what to do with those months. As it
happened I heard in Cambridge that Wittgenstein, who
was no longer there,[46] was having difficulty in finding a
good translator for *Philosophische Untersuchungen*, so I
decided to write and offer to try to translate it. In my
letter I told him I had heard that he was having difficulty
in finding a good translator, that I had five months to
spare before entering chambers and that I could not
think of a better way of spending those months than in
trying to translate his book. Remembering, however, his

[45] I was already well acquainted with the impressive words of
Berkeley: 'Whatever the world may opine, he who hath not much
meditated upon God, the human mind, and the *summum bonum*, may
possibly make a thriving earth-worm, but will most indubitably make
a blundering patriot and a sorry statesman.' Yet this passage itself, if
it implies action as well as reflection, may well be setting *too* high a
moral standard for politicians, who surely need not be saints for them
to confer great benefits on their countries and even on the world at
large.
[46] He had resigned the Chair of Philosophy late in 1947 and was in
Eire doing philosophical work.

avowed principle that people should be properly paid for what they do, I added that I would need to ask him to give me a fair fee for doing the work.

It was not long before I had a reply, but it was not at all the reply that I had hoped for. It was pretty curt. Wittgenstein said I had been misinformed, and that in any case he could not afford to pay a translator.[47] I was not only disappointed, but peeved at the tone of his letter. Yet I really had little right to be, as I had not contacted him for some years, and I was not very anxious to come under his personal domination, or even to get back to intensive philosophical discussions with him, had that been possible. I spent part of the months translating two books of Ockham's *Summa Totius Logicae*. I was fascinated with the controversy between Nominalism and Realism, and by the possibility that Ockham was rather a Conceptualist about Universals than a Nominalist. These topics actually had quite close connexions with certain central topics in Wittgenstein's work, so that vicarious contact was not utterly broken. Indeed I suspected that that huge controversy, on which such subtle brains in the middle ages had expended such energy, would have been amenable to dissolution by a rigorous application of Wittgenstein's philosophical method, and I would have been more than superficially interested in seeing exactly how that could be done.

[47] I have been trying to find his letter among my hoard of old papers; but have not so far found it. I *may* have simply destroyed it in my disappointment, but I doubt that.

30

The last time I actually met Wittgenstein was in a barber's shop in Trinity Street. He was having his hair cut in one of the seats and I was just about to have mine cut in a nearby one. I greeted him and he greeted me. I believe this was early in 1949 when I was about half-way through my pupilage at the Bar. He asked me what I was doing and I told him. He said he thought it an immensely difficult thing to be a Judge. I said that that was my impression too, but that a Judge was something I might well never be and what I was to have to do in the more immediate future was to help my Master in Chambers to prepare cases and go with him to the High Court and accompany another member of the chambers to County Courts. I would also later probably go on Circuit. He seemed vague about what Circuit was, but I had no time to explain. I was in a hurry and had to leave the shop. As I did so I called out cheerily, thinking of older days: 'Give me a ring some time!' His response was not at all friendly, and he seemed to be muttering something to himself of a deprecatory kind. Anyway, I never had a telephone call from him, and my momentary impulse of friendliness was not sustained. In any case I was scarcely in Cambridge during the rest of 1949, except at week-ends, and my father, who had had a welcome spell in the winter of 1948-1949 with my mother at Menton, had come back in poor health, and my mother was far from well too. They had been driven back home by my old friend Roland Cailleux,[48] who was a medical specialist.

[48] Roland Cailleux was also a novelist of distinction. His best known novels are *Saint-Genès ou la vie brève*, Paris 1943, and *À moi-même inconnu*, Paris 1978.

My father had a most wretched time in hospital from May and died in August 1949. I had become engaged in June 1949 to marry a charming Irish girl. So I had other things and people to think about besides Wittgenstein and any possible renewal of contact with him.[49]

I did *see* him again, nearly two years later, in the spring of 1951. I was by now myself a Fellow of Trinity, having been elected from 1 October 1950 and appointed an Assistant Lecturer at Trinity in English (Literature). One fine sunny morning I happened to be visiting one of my pupils who had rooms overlooking Trinity Street, and as we both stood looking out of the window I was surprised to see Wittgenstein walking slowly along the pavement on the opposite side of the road. He looked pale and ill, but his head was not bowed and his fine features showed impressively as he looked upwards on that bright morning. I had a presentiment that it might well be not all that long before he died. I had been busy preparing my new classes, and had also had various other preoccupations. It was not therefore so surprising that I had not heard of Wittgenstein's terminal illness, or the wonderful kindness of Dr and Mrs Bevan in saving him from the possibility of dying in hospital by taking him into their house in Storey's Way and caring for him there. Knowing nothing of this, all I saw was the frail relic of the remarkable man towards whom I had felt often warmly, though often ambivalently, in those earlier years until about ten years before, but by whom I had felt rather harshly rebuffed more recently about my

[49]Joan Bevan, who talked a good deal with Wittgenstein towards the end of his life, has told me that he said that I had been a friend of his, but had been much changed by my time in the army. How *could* he have arrived at such a conclusion? (Cf. his similar initial reaction to Drury after a long absence; but in that case his friendly feelings soon reasserted themselves. See M.O'C. Drury, 'Conversations with Wittgenstein' in op. cit, ed. Rush Rhees, Oxford 1981, pp. 161-2.)

translation offer and coolly treated at the barber's shop. As I watched him walk slowly along I was far from devoid of feeling. Indeed my feelings were strong and painfully conflicting, and I was quite perplexed as to what to *do*. I was sad to see him looking so very ill. I even thought it might be a shock to him if I suddenly rushed down and went up to him. But nor did I want to be rebuffed. And there were other things that went through my head: I didn't want to get deeply involved again, or even to look after him. I didn't know where he was living – I had heard Oxford, I had heard Ireland. I doubted whether there was anything to be gained for him or for me by making contact again. There were other people I cared for much more than I did for him, despite the fact that my admiration for his philosophy and his philosophical method, and the force of his personality and of his writing, remained (and always will remain) as strong as ever. The result was that I did absolutely nothing, and only heard, about a fortnight later, that he had died in the Bevans' house. It is possible that if I had known as much as I do now about the terrible experiences that had formed part of what he finally called his 'wonderful life', I might at least have tried to make some of his last moments more pleasurable, had opportunity really offered. But who can tell?

Appendix

Dear Dr Wittgenstein,

I wonder if you will be so kind as to clear up a difficulty which I experience with regard to Mr Hardie's[1] question in your lecture this afternoon.

Let us consider the case of a quotient with a decimal period of (say) 50 places (recurring at the 51st place). Then, if I do not know that it is decimally periodic, suppose someone asks me: 'Is there a 7 in the infinite development of this division?' Suppose I develop the division up to 55 places (say), *and* that I 'discover periodicity', then suppose I am asked the same question again: 'Is there a 7 in the infinite development of this division?', I am tempted to believe that the meaning of the question has *changed*, *if* there is in fact *no* 7 in the first period of 50 places, but that it has *not* changed *if* there *is* in fact a 7 in the first period of 50 places. And I am tempted to believe this for the following reasons:

Suppose I calculate just to 50 places and stop before calculating the 51st place; and that I do not know that these 50 places are in fact the first period of a periodic decimal. If there is *no* 7 in these first 50 places I shall be

---

[1] Charles Hardie (BA Magdalene 1934, MA 1943). He ultimately taught Philosophy at the University of Tasmania. I believe that Charles Hardie's question was whether the *meaning* of the question 'Is there a 7 in the infinite development of a division of one integer by another integer?' changes if one at some point 'discovers periodicity'.

as perplexed by the question 'Is there a 7 in the infinite development of this division?' as I was before I started the calculation. I may in fact say: 'Oh! how long does he expect me to go on?' or something of that sort. If, however, I knew that these 50 places which I had calculated were the first period of a periodic decimal, and there was *no* 7 in those 50 places, I should then be inclined to say 'No' to the question 'Is there a 7 in the infinite development of this division?' because I can't help accepting the being or not being of a digit in a period of a quotient as a criterion for the respective being or not being of a digit in an infinite development of the division of which the period is part of the quotient. Whereas, if I calculate just to 50 places, and stop before calculating the 51st place, and do not know that these 50 places are in fact the first period of a periodic decimal, AND IF THERE *IS* a 7 in these 50 places, I shall not be perplexed, but shall answer 'Yes' to the question 'Is there a 7 in the infinite development of this division?' If I know the first 50 places to be a period I shall still answer 'Yes' to the question 'Is there a 7 in the infinite development?'

It *seems* to me therefore that the meaning of the question CHANGES if there is *no* 7 in the first period of 50 places, from the meaning it had when I didn't know that those 50 places constituted a period; to the meaning it has when I do know this: WHEREAS if there *is* a 7 in the first period of 50 places the meaning the question had when I didn't know that these 50 places constituted a period is the same as when I do know that they do.

If you could clear this difficulty up for me I should be most grateful.

Yours sincerely,
Theodore Redpath

Index

Index

Index